Fundamentals 1

Answer Key

℘ Cover Art by Claire Yanoschick ℘

Mother of Divine Grace School

Ojai, CA

© 2014

Item #041

❧ Table of Contents ❧

Lesson I
ఆ◌ఇ

Practice Exercises

A. Underline all nouns in the following passage:

<u>Alexander</u> studied the <u>behavior</u> of the <u>horse</u>. <u>Alexander</u> saw <u>fear</u> in the <u>horse</u>. <u>Alexander</u> realized the <u>horse</u> was terrified of <u>shadows</u>. <u>Alexander</u> turned the <u>horse</u> so the terrified <u>animal</u> couldn't see the <u>shadow</u> and the <u>horse</u> became a peaceful <u>giant</u>.

B. Match each noun to the correct type:

truth (abstract)	abstract
Taj Majal (proper)	regular
food (regular)	proper
girl (regular)	collective
army (collective)	regular
Mary Wells (proper)	abstract
love (abstract)	proper
lizard (regular)	regular

Practice Exercises

C. Give the plurals of the following nouns:

a. cow	<u>cows</u>
b. ox	<u>oxen</u>
c. fox	<u>foxes</u>
d. itch	<u>itches</u>
e. sky	<u>skies</u>
f. child	<u>children</u>
g. pie	<u>pies</u>
h. radio	<u>radios</u>
i. tomato	<u>tomatoes</u>

D. Come up with your own list of the following:

(Answers may vary)

3 Common Nouns:

_____

3 Proper Nouns:

_____ *100%*

3 Collective Nouns:

_____

3 Abstract Nouns:

_____

Additional Exercises

A. Form the plural of the following nouns:

a. woman   <u>women</u>
b. cat   <u>cats</u>
c. box   <u>boxes</u>
d. sandwich   <u>sandwiches</u>   *100%*   *Done Sept 7th*
e. wish   <u>wishes</u>
f. inch   <u>inches</u>
g. try   <u>tries</u>

B. Say whether the underlined nouns are common or proper.

a. <u>Samantha</u> and her <u>cat</u> named <u>Halley</u> won the <u>show</u>.
<u>Samantha — proper, cat — common, Halley — proper, show — common</u>

b. I wanted to watch the <u>television</u>, but <u>Mark</u> wanted to play <u>baseball</u>.   *100%*
<u>television — common, Mark — proper, baseball — common</u>

c. The <u>Smiths</u> are <u>friends</u> of the <u>family</u> who lives down the gated <u>road</u>.
<u>Smiths — proper, friends — common, family — common, road — common</u>

C. Say whether the nouns below are regular, abstract or collective. Of course, they are all common.

a. joy   abstract
b. team   collective
c. society   collective
d. apple   regular
e. ocean   regular
f. angel   regular
g. army   collective
h. ice cream   regular

100%

D. Underline all nouns in the following exercise. Say whether each is common or proper. If it is common, specify also whether it is regular, abstract or collective.

a. The whistle of the parrot confirmed the existence of the pirates.
  whistle — common, regular; parrot — common, regular; existence — common,
  abstract; pirates — common, regular

6/8

b. The army had to be called out to defeat the enemy. army
— common, collective; enemy — common, collective   ✓

c. The men worked as a team.
  men — common, regular; team — common, collective   3/2

d. The crew of the ship was driven back to the sea.
  crew — common, collective; ship — common, regular; sea — common, regular   ✓

e. The brigade won under the leadership of the brilliant generals, especially
  General Jones.
brigade — common, collective; leadership — common, abstract; generals —
common, regular; General Jones — proper   4/5

Lesson II
ဩ၁ဨ

Practice Exercises

A. Find the complete predicate in the following sentences. Underline the complete predicate once. Then find the simple predicate (the verb) in the following sentences. Underline them twice.

(simple predicate is boxed)

a. Both sides wanted the prize.
b. The pitcher ran to home base.
c. The catcher sent him back to the mound.
d. The poor pitcher is confused.
e. The pitcher did not want the batter on his home base. ✓
f. He threw a fastball.
g. The batter swung.
h. Swing the bat!

B. Find the simple subject in the following sentences. Circle the simple subjects. The key is to first find the simple predicate and then ask yourself "who" or "what" about the simple predicate.

a. The boy kicked the ball. Who or what "kicked"? boy
(The answer is the subject).
b. The boy seems happy.   Who or what "seems" happy? boy
c. The child calls to the dog. Who or what "calls" the dog? child ✓
d. Arthur rode the horse.   Who or what "rode" the horse? Arthur
e. The cat growled at the dog.   Who or what "growled" at the dog? cat

B. Underline the complete subjects once and the simple subjects twice.

(simple subjects are boxed)

a. Sasha and Timothy ran to the store.
b. My aunt Jemima makes great pancakes.
c. Lunchtime in our house is exciting. ✓
d. A great storyteller demands perfect silence.
e. Down the road in a small house lives a happy family.

4

C. Underline all verbs in the following:

Many people <u>enjoy</u> our fourth of July holiday. But how many of them <u>remember</u> what it <u>is</u> really about? Why <u>have</u> we <u>chosen</u> the fourth of July? We <u>celebrate</u> independence from England on that day. We <u>celebrate</u> the men and women whose determination <u>made</u> our country great. We <u>celebrate</u> the men and women whose loyalty <u>kept</u> it strong and safe.

Additional Exercises

A. Underline all nouns in the following:

In the <u>year</u> that is now famous, <u>Columbus</u> and his <u>men</u> set out for the <u>Indies</u>. Several <u>months</u> later they landed in a <u>place</u> they thought was the <u>Indies</u>. It turns out it was in the <u>Caribbean</u> and was quite far away from the <u>Indies</u>.

B. Underline the simple subjects in the following:

a. A big <u>parade</u> was held.
b. The <u>men</u> of the town were blocking the road.
c. The <u>soldiers</u> got to their vehicles in time.
d. The <u>boys</u> and <u>girls</u> of the town enjoyed the show.
e. The <u>weather</u> is really hot.
f. <u>Thomas Jefferson</u> sent Louis and Clark on an expedition.
g.

C. Underline the simple subject once and the simple verb twice.

(simple verbs are boxed)

a. Large and gaily painted <u>gondolas</u> drifted on the river's waters.
b. <u>Trumpets</u> heralded the arrival of the king.
c. The <u>music</u>, growing soft and slow, came to a halt.
d. From behind the door, <u>Mary</u> could see the workman.
e. My <u>heroes</u> are not athletes, but saints.

5

D. Notice the subject is always the "who" or "what" of the verb, but not always the one doing the action. Active verbs have subjects doing action. Passive verbs have subjects receiving action. Active and passive are voices.

a. The cake **is baked** by Mary.   (Passive voice: Cake is receiving the baking.)

Who or what is baked? cake (answer to this is the subject.)

Who or what did the baking? Mary (answer isn't the subject.)

b. Mary **bakes** the cake.   (Active voice: Mary is doing the baking.)

Who or what bakes? Mary (answer to this is the subject.)

Who or what did the baking? Mary (answer is the subject.)

Lesson III
ဆေ၃

Practice Exercises

A. Answer these questions

a. What are the five things that a verb conjugation expresses?
mood, tense, voice, person, and number.

b. What are the three things that a noun declension expresses?
gender, number, and case.

c. How many conjugations are there in Latin?
four

d. How many declensions are there in Latin?
five

e. You decline Latin verbs. True or False?
False. You conjugate Latin verbs. You decline Latin nouns.

B. Identify the conjugation of the following words:

a. orāre first   b. agere third

c. laudāre first   d. ponere third

e. tenēre second   f. petere third

g. audīre fourth   h. contendere third

i. munīre fourth   j. occupāre first

Practice Exercises

C. Identify the stem of the following words:

a. orāre ora   b. agere age

c. laudāre lauda   d. ponere pone

e. tenēre tene   f. petere pete

g. audīre audi   h. contendere contende

i. munīre muni   j. occupāre occupa

7

Additional Exercises

A. Underline all simple nouns in the following passage. Circle all that are used as subjects. Double underline all simple predicates.

(simple predicates are boxed)

Out of all boys, Albert most observed the world around him. Albert studied the birds of the air, the plants, and the insects. Science excited him. Albert saw God's hand and direction in all things. Thomas Aquinas was wise in choosing* him as a teacher.

*Choosing should be ignored.

B. Begin to memorize the new vocabulary. Look up the meaning in your glossary:

a. orāre to pray   b. agere to do, act

c. laudāre to praise   d. ponere to put, place

e. tenēre to hold   f. petere to seek

g. audīre to hear   h. contendere to hasten

i. munīre to build   j. occupāre to seize

C. Identify the tense of each of the following:

(The tenses are past, present and future)

a. I am calling the number.	present
b. The guest will arrive in an hour.	future
c. Be calm, please.	present
d. I ran to the store yesterday.	past

D. Identify the mood of each of the following:

The moods are: indicative/declarative (a statement/question), imperative (a command), subjunctive (a wish or something contrary to fact).

a. Jump.	imperative
b. Stop that at once!	imperative
c. If I were going, I would help.	subjunctive
d. I asked for the green cup.	indicative
e. The blueberries are ripe.	indicative

8

Lesson IV

෨ඏ

Practice Exercises

A. Suppose the following verbs are going to be put into Latin. What person and number do each one show? (1st Person, 2nd Person, 3rd Person? Singular Number, Plural Number?)

a. <u>They</u> are.   3rd Person   Plural Number

b. <u>She</u> is running.   3rd Person   Singular Number

c. I act.   1st Person   Singular Number

d. Boys, <u>you</u> must come now.   2nd Person   Plural Number

e. <u>You</u> are nice, Jane.   2nd Person   Singular Number

f. <u>It</u> is red.   3rd Person   Singular Number

g. <u>We</u> will eat.   1st Person   Plural Number

B. Give the Latin ending you would use for each of the following:

a. we mus   b. I   o or m   c. you (sing)   s   d. he   t

e. it   t   f. she t   g. you (plural) tis   h. they nt

C. Choose whether the following actions are complete or incomplete:

a. I will call.   Complete   Incomplete

b. You did hold.   Complete   Incomplete

c. We are eating.   Complete   Incomplete

d. He does sing.   Complete   Incomplete

e. The rose is growing.   Complete   Incomplete

f. The dog has eaten dinner.   Complete   Incomplete

D. Mark with a ☑☑ any sentence that contains the verb "to be" used alone, that is, not as a helping verb.

___We are writing letters.

X You were there.

X Monica is happiest.

___Thomas is eating a cake.

Additional Exercises

A. Underline the simple predicate:

a. John <u>is calling</u> for his sister.

b. A friend <u>is</u> with us.

c. She <u>is running</u> to the dock.

d. We <u>are</u> so happy for the family.

B. Begin to memorize this new vocabulary. Circle the stems. Look up the meaning in your glossary:

a. mittere <u>to send</u>

c. dicere   <u>to speak</u>

e. credere <u>to believe</u>

g. venire   <u>to come</u>

i. cedere   <u>to yield</u>

b. bibere <u>to drink</u>

d. ducere <u>to lead</u>

f. currere <u>to run</u>

 h. discere <u>to learn</u>

C. Underline every subject in the following sentences:

<u>John</u> ate cake at the party. <u>He</u> has a good time at parties. His <u>friends</u> enjoy the party too. <u>They</u> love parties. <u>They</u> wish for more cake. Chocolate <u>cake (or "chocolate cake")</u> is a favorite. Many <u>cakes</u> are favorites.

D. What personal ending (person and number) would each verb take? Underline the verb and then give its person and number:

a. We <u>trust</u> the state.	Person: 1st	Number: plural
b. It <u>haunts</u> the sport.	Person: 3rd	Number: singular
c. You, teammates, <u>prevent</u> injuries.	Person: 2nd	Number: plural
d. I <u>enjoy</u> a good game.	Person: <u>1st</u>	Number: <u>singular</u>

Lesson V

ℬⅅℭℜ

Practice Exercises

A. Translate the following Latin words into English. Remember they are present:

a. credo	I believe (am believing/do believe)
b. credis	you believe (are believing/do believe)
c. credit	he (she, it) believes (etc)
d. credimus	we believe
e. creditis	you (pl) believe
f. credunt	they believe

B. Translate the following English phrases into Latin.

Example: a. I seek   Stem: pete +o   peto[1]

b. you seek	Stem: pete +s	petis[2]
c. he seeks	Stem: pete +t	petit
d. we seek	Stem: pete +mus	petimus
e. you (pl) seek	Stem: pete +tis	petitis
f. they seek[5]	Stem: pete +nt	petunt

C. Say whether each of the following is emphatic present, progressive present, or simple present:

a. They do call us every week.	emphatic present
b. I wonder.	simple present
c. He does say that often.	emphatic present
d. You are calling, right?	progressive present
e. What do you like best?	emphatic present

---

[1] Remember, the first person singular is irregular. The "e" is dropped from the stem, and the first person singular ending, "o," is added.

[2] Remember to change the "e" of the stem to "i"

[3] Remember, the third person plural is irregular.

D. Identify the person (1, 2, 3) and number (Sing, Plur) of the underlined words:

a. <u>We</u> ran the race.   <u>1st person, plural</u>

b. <u>You</u> should all come.   <u>2nd person, plural</u>

c. <u>She</u> said what?   <u>3rd person, singular</u>

d. <u>Mary</u> said what?   <u>3rd person, singular</u>

e. <u>They</u> came to tea.   <u>3rd person, plural</u>

Additional Exercises

A. Replace all underlined nouns with pronouns in the following sentences. Use these pronouns only: he, she, it, they, we, you:

a. <u>John</u> is happy.   <u>He</u>

b. <u>My friends and I</u> ran to town.   <u>We</u>

c. <u>Child,</u> come here.   <u>You</u>

d. The <u>dog</u> wagged its tail.   <u>It</u>

e. The dog ate <u>food</u>.   <u>It</u>

B. Mark with a ☑☑ any sentence which contains the verb "to be" used alone, that is, not as a helping verb:

__We are asking for help.

<u>X</u> You are happy.

__They have called.

<u>X</u> God is.

C. Identify the verbs as expressing complete or incomplete action and as past, present or future:

a. Michael is seeking assistance.　　☐☐ complete　　☐☐ incomplete
Tense: present

b. I have called the agent.　　☐☐ complete　　☐☐ incomplete
Tense: present

c. I had called the park office.　　☐☐ complete　　☐☐ incomplete
Tense: past

d. I will ask the ranger.　　☐☐ complete　　☐☐ incomplete
Tense: future

e. I teach math.　　☐☐ complete　　☐☐ incomplete
Tense: present

f. I taught math.　　☐☐ complete　　☐☐ incomplete
Tense: present

D. In the above exercise, every place you checked the word "complete", please cross out "complete" and write "perfect system" above it. Every place you checked the word "incomplete," please cross out "incomplete" and put "present system" above it.

Lesson VI
৶৹ন্দ্র

Practice Exercises

A. Replace the subject with a pronoun. The first one is done for you:

a. <u>Mary</u> exercised the dog.　　<u>She</u> exercised the dog.
　　　　　　　　　　　　　　3rd person, singular　　　　　　"t"

b. <u>The children</u> were laughing.　<u>They</u> were laughing,
　　　　　　　　　　　　　　3rd person, plural　　　　　　nt

c. <u>The boy</u> ran a lap.　　　　<u>He</u> ran a lap.
　　　　　　　　　　　　　　3rd person, singular　　　　　　t

d. <u>The happy dog</u> barked.　　<u>It</u> barked.
　　　　　　　　　　　　　　3rd person, singular　　　　　　t

B. You now have ways to identify nouns and verbs. Circle the ending that would be identified with verbs:

---ei　　　　---re　　　　---us　　　　---i　　　　---ae　　　　---is

C. Identify the declension of the following words:

a. victoria, victoriae	1st	2nd	3rd	4th	5th
b. donum, doni	1st	2nd	3rd	4th	5th
c. virtus, virtutis	1st	2nd	3rd	4th	5th
d. dies, diei	1st	2nd	3rd	4th	5th
e. pastor, pastoris	1st	2nd	3rd	4th	5th
f. mare, maris	1st	2nd	3rd	4th	5th
g. portus, portus	1st	2nd	3rd	4th	5th

D. Identify the <u>stem</u> of the following words:

a. victoria, victoriae   <u>victori</u>

b. donum, doni   <u>don</u>

c. virtus, virtutis   <u>virtut</u>

d. dies, diei   <u>di</u>

e. pastor, pastoris   <u>pastor</u>

f. mare, maris   <u>mar</u>

g. portus, portus   <u>port</u>

Additional Exercises

A. Give the meaning for each of the following verbs:

a. orāre <u>to pray</u>   b. agere <u>to do, act</u>

c. laudāre <u>to praise</u>   d. ponere <u>to put, place</u>

e. tenēre <u>to hold</u>   f. petere <u>to seek</u>

g. audīre <u>to hear</u>   h. contendere <u>to hasten</u>

i. munīre <u>to build</u>   j. occupāre <u>to seize</u>

k. mittere <u>to send</u>   l. bibere <u>to drink</u>

m. dicere <u>to speak</u>   n. ducere <u>to lead</u>

o. credere <u>to believe</u>   p. currere <u>to run</u>

q. venīre <u>to come</u>   r. discere <u>to learn</u>

B. Translate the following Latin words into English. Remember they are present:

a. dico   <u>I speak</u>

b. dicis   <u>you speak</u>

c. mittit   <u>he (she, it) speaks</u>

d. mittimus   <u>we speak</u>

e. ponitis   <u>you (pl) speak</u>

f. ponunt   <u>they speak</u>

C. Translate the following English phrases into Latin:

a. I seek   Stem: pete + o   peto[1]
b. You believe   Stem: crede +s   credis[2]
c. He sends   Stem: mitte +t   mittit
d. We do   Stem: age +mus   agimus
e. You (pl) drink   Stem: bibe +tis   bibitis
f. They learn   Stem: disce +nt   discunt

D. The word for king is "rex, regis" in Latin. The first form is the nominative form. Please underline it. Nominatives equal subjects. Now, translate the sentences:

a. The king rules.   Stem: rege + t

NOUN + VERB   rex + regit

b. The king does.   Stem: age + t

NOUN + VERB   rex + agit

c. The king sends.   Stem: mitte + t

NOUN + VERB   rex + mittit

---

[1] Remember the first form is irregular. The "e" of the stem is dropped and just "o" is added.
[2] Remember to change the "e" of the stem" to "i"

Lesson VII

ಬಿ‌ಐ

Practice Exercises

A. Which of the following is an infinitive? Mark with a ☑☑ any sentence which contains an infinitive:

X   a. I want to eat.

___   b. I seek a path to the mountain.

X   c. I want to seek a path to the mountain.

___   d. To the store, we go.

B. Please cross all articles out in this paragraph:

~~The~~ quick brown fox jumped over ~~the~~ lazy dog. ~~The~~ fox was very fast and very fit. ~~The~~ dog was both ~~a~~ lazy dog and ~~a~~ fat dog. ~~The~~ dog was ~~a~~ sad dog when ~~the~~ fox jumped over him.

C. Review. Please fill in the blanks:

a. To get the present tense for verbs, you drop the "re," change the <u>e</u> to i and add the endings.

b." You" is <u>2nd</u> person, plural.

c. "I" is the 1st person, <u>singular</u>.

d. <u>"They"</u> is the 3rd person, plural.

e. "We" is the first person, <u>plural</u>.

f. The three ways of expressing the present tense are: <u>simple</u>, progressive, and <u>emphatic</u>.

g. How do you recognize an English infinitive? A Latin one? <u>An English infinitive is a verb word preceded by "to." A Latin infinitive is a verb word ending in "re."</u>

D. Compose your own sentences, using one of the following in each:

(answers may vary)

a. Collective noun:

_____

b. Completed action in the past:

_____

c. Your name as subject:

_____

d. A verb that is 2nd person, plural:

_____

Additional Exercises

A. Mark off the stems of these verbs:

cedere --- to yield

agere --- to do, act

laudare --- to praise

bibere --- to drink

venire --- to come

ponere --- to put, place

contendere --- to hasten

tenere --- to hold

mittere --- to send

ducere --- to lead

discere --- to learn

petere --- to seek

munire --- to fortify

audire --- to hear

dicere to speak

currere to run

credere --- to believe

B. Give the Latin endings that go with these English pronouns:

a. you (sing) <u>s</u>

c. I   <u>o or m</u>

e. we   <u>mus</u>

g. she   <u>t</u>

b. you (pl)   <u>tis</u>

d. they   <u>nt</u>

f. he   <u>t</u>

h. it   <u>t</u>

C. Give the meaning of the following nouns. Use your glossary. Circle the stems:

a. pars, partis   part
b. virtus, virtutis   virtue
c. dux, ducis   leader
d. rex, regis   king
e. gens, gentis   tribe
f. arbor, arboris   tree
g. caput, capitis   head
h. agmen, agminis   column, army
i. Caesar, Caesaris   Caesar
j. canis, canis   dog
k. Cicero, Ciceronis   Cicero
l. caritas, caritatis   love

D. Matching

a. first form (nominative)   Nominative
b. I do call. (emphatic)   Progressive
c. I call. (simple)   Emphatic
d. I am calling. (progressive)   Simple

Lesson VIII
ഐൽ

Practice Exercises

A. Translate the following Latin words into English. Remember they are past:

a. credebam — I was believing

b. credebas — you were believing

c. credebat — he (she, it) was believing

d. credebamus — we were believing

e. credebatis — you (pl) were believing

f. credebant — they were believing

B. Translate the following English phrases into Latin:

a. I was doing — Stem: _age_ + _ba_ +m — agebam

b. you were doing — Stem: age + ba +s — agebas

c. he was doing — Stem: age + ba +t — agebat

d. we were doing — Stem: age + ba +mus — agebamus

e. you (pl) were doing — Stem: age + ba +tis — agebatis

f. they were doing — Stem: age + ba +nt — agebant

C. Fill in this chart with the Latin forms of the verb "to be":

	Singular (one)	Plural (more than one)
1st Person (I, we)	sum	sumus
2nd Person (you, you (pl.))	es	estis
3rd Person (he,she,it, they)	est	sunt

D. Take the verb forms given here and circle the endings. Say what pronoun goes with the ending:

VERB	PRONOUN	PERSON	NUMBER
Example:			
a. cred<u>o</u>	I	1st Person	Singular
b. pone<u>bamus</u>	we	1st	plural
c. bib<u>it</u>	he (she, it)	3rd	singular
d. duce<u>batis</u>	you (pl)	2nd	plural
e. est<u>is</u>	you (pl)	2nd	plural
f. es<u>t</u>	he (she, it)	3rd	singular
g. dic<u>unt</u>	they	3rd	plural

Additional Exercises

A. Mark with a ☑☑ any sentence which contains the verb "to be" used alone (not as a helping verb). Then double underline all the verbs and their pronouns in the sentences:

X   a. <u>I</u> <u>am</u> very happy about the victory.

_____ b. <u>I am learning</u> a lot.

_____ c. <u>You</u> (pl) <u>were believing</u> us.

_____ d. <u>We are putting</u> you in charge.

X   e. <u>He is</u> lively.

B. Translate the above verbs. Remember for the sentences using the verb "to be" just look back in the lesson to the new irregular word:

a. <u>sum</u>

b. <u>disco</u>

c. <u>credebatis</u>

d. <u>ponimus</u>

e. <u>est</u>

C. Put the letter that corresponds to each sentence in the correct box for that sentence:

f. I was baking a cake.

g. I am baking a cake.

h. I will have eaten the cake.

i. I have run to the store.

j. I had eaten the pie.

k. I baked a cake.

g. I will laugh.

h. I call.

i. I will have taken the car.

j. I had baked a pie before this.

k. I am laughing.

l. I have just eaten the cake.

	INCOMPLETE ACTIONS	COMPLETE ACTIONS
PRESENT	b, h, k	d, f, l
PAST	a	e, j
FUTURE	g	c, i

D. Translate the following sentences. Remember the first form of the noun in Latin is the nominative:

a. Virtue was ruling.   Stem: rege + ba + t

  NOUN + VERB   virtus + regebat

b. The shepherd puts.   Stem: pone + t

  NOUN + VERB   pastor + ponit [1]

c. The tribe is.   NA
  NOUN + VERB   gens + est

---
[1] Remember to change the "e" to "i" in the present.

23

Review I & Culture Study

ಲ಄ಐ

Practice Exercises

A. Put the months into the right boxes (use the rhyme "30 days hath September)":

Month with 31 Days	Month with 30 Days	Month with 28 Days
January	September	February
March	April	
May	June	
July	November	
August		
October		
December		

B. Answer These

The Nones are on what day in…

July	7th
March	7th
April	5th
September	5th

The ides are on what day in…

July	15th
March	15th
April	13th
September	13th

24

C. What day is…

AD XV Kalends July   June 17

Dec 25   VIII Kalends January

March 12   IV Ides March

Figure out your Birthday: (answers may vary)

D. Answer These

156 AUC would be   598 B. C.

1154 AUC would be 400 A.D.

Additional Exercises

A. Underline all nouns in the following paragraph <u>once</u>; underline all verbs <u>twice.</u> Write "S" above all subjects:

(verbs are boxed; subjects are in parentheses)

(Solomon) reigns in his glory. The (Queen) from Sheba tests his wisdom. Before him, the (Queen) sets two flowers. The (flowers) are lovely. The (Queen) tells him these words. "(You) choose the real flower." (King Solomon) sees a bee. (It) will help him. The (bee) flies to one flower. The (bee) gave him the answer.

B. Circle the stems of the following words. Mark "N" for nouns and "V" for verbs:

N caritas, caritatis	V ponere	N caritas, caritatis
N pater, patris	N Caesar, Caesaris	V petere
V regere	V contendere	V munire
V laudare	V tenere	N canis, canis
V credere	N caput, capitis	V sum
N arbor, arboris	V dicere	N agmen, agminis
N gens, gentis	V ducere	V currere

C. Mark each sentence that uses the verb "to be" alone:

_____ I am calling the pizza place.

X   Sarah was sad.

_____ The men were happily working.

X   That cat is pretty.

X   Patricia is my pet penguin's name.

_____ The computer is not computing properly.

D. Take the verb forms given here and circle the endings. Say what pronoun goes with the ending. Give a translation:

VERB	PRONOUN	PERSON	NUMBER	TRANSLATE
a. credo	I	1st	Sing	I believe
b. dicebamus	we	1st	Pl	we were speaking
c. bibebatis	you (pl)	2nd	Pl	you were drinking
d. es	yo	2nd	Sing	you are
e. ponis	yo	2nd	Sing	you put
f. sum	I	1st	Sing	I am
g. aget	he (she, it)	3rd	Sing	He does

Lesson IX

ॐ

Practice Exercises

A. Which of these sentences use the verb "to be" alone? ☑☑ them:

____ In a busy store, the salesmen were working.

____They did not eat their lunch.

____They ordered pizza for lunch.

____They never got it.

X   The pizza guy was in their store!

X   The salesmen were pretty hungry men that day!

B. Which of these sentences have a direct object or predicate nominative? ☑☑ them. (Remember they answer the question whom or what about the action or state of being of the subject.)

____ In a busy store, the salesmen were working.

X   They did not eat their lunch.

X   They ordered pizza for lunch.

X   They never got it.

____ The pizza guy was in their store!

X   The salesmen were pretty hungry men that day!

C. Which one of the sentences above has a predicate nominative in it? The salesmen were pretty hungry men that day! "Men" is the predicate nominative.

D. Some verbs naturally seem to always want a direct object, some don't. Circle any of the following verbs that usually take a direct object. The first one is done for you:

(Hint: Use the "whom or what" trick. Make two or three sentences with the verb and ask yourself "whom or what" about the action of the subject. If there is no answer, then it is probably a verb that doesn't take a direct object.)

a. yell

I yell loudly. (I yell whom or what? There is no answer.)

I yell at the dog. (I yell whom or what? There is no answer — the "at" is necessary; I can't say, "I yell the dog.")

So "yell" is not circled.

b. discover

c. believe

d. roll

Feb. 17th, 2017

e. argue

f. live

28

Additional Exercises

A. Underline all direct objects in the below paragraph and circle any subjects or predicate nominatives:

(subjects/predicate nominatives are boxed)

The [branches] of geology include some interesting <u>ones</u>. [Physical Geology] and [Physical Oceanography] are two [branches] that are well known. [Geophysics] is the [science] that interests <u>me</u> most. This [science] includes the <u>study</u> of earthquakes.

B. Mark all nouns in the paragraph below, then say how they are used. (That is, are they direct objects? Subjects? Predicate Nominatives?)

The Revolutionary War was a great war. France helped America. America paid her debt later. The Americans helped the French win World War II. French men were German captives. America freed the captives.

(Do not take points off if student included "French" with "men" or "German" with "captives.")

Revolutionary War — subject	French — direct object
war — predicate nominative	World War II — direct object
France — subject	men — subject
America — direct object	captives — predicate nominative
America — subject	America — subject
debt — direct object	captives — direct
object Americans — subject	

C. Give the stem and the meaning of the following words. Circle the Nominative/First form.

a. nomen, nominis   Stem: <u>nomin</u>   Meaning: <u>name</u>

b. vox, vocis   Stem: <u>voc</u>   Meaning: <u>voice</u>

c. veritas, veritatis   Stem: <u>veritat</u>   Meaning: <u>truth</u>

d. urbs, urbis   Stem: <u>urb</u>   Meaning: <u>city</u>

e. lex, legis   Stem: <u>leg</u>   Meaning: <u>law</u>

f. lux, lucis   Stem: <u>luc</u>   Meaning: <u>light</u>

g. eques, equitis   Stem: <u>equit</u>   Meaning: <u>horseman</u>

D. Fill out the charts below using the verb "agere."

This is the PRESENT chart. To fill it out remember the following: take the stem, change "e" to "i" and add the personal endings (o, s, t, mus, tis, nt). The irregular ones are already done for you.

STEM: age	Singular	Plural
1st Person	**ago/I do, I act**	agimus/we do, we act
2nd Person	agis/you do, you act	agitis/you (pl) do, you act
3rd Person	agit/he does, he acts (she, it)	**agunt/they do, they act**

This is the PAST chart. To fill it out remember the following: take the stem, add a "ba" to the end of it, and then add the personal endings (m, s, t, mus, tis, nt).

STEM: age	Singular	Plural
1st Person	agebam/I was doing, I was acting	agebamus/we were doing, we were acting
2nd Person	agebas/you were doing, you were acting	agebatis/you (pl) were doing, you were acting
3rd Person	agebat/he was doing, he was acting (she, it)	agebant/they were doing, they were acting

Lesson X

Ɛ❀Ɔ

Practice Exercises

A. Fill in the chart:

Latin Word	Gender	Predicate Nominative Form (same as Nominative first Form)	Stem (Second form minus "is")	Accusative Form (Stem + em) Same as nominatve if neuter
pater, patris	m	pater	patr	patrem
dux, ducis	m	dux	duc	ducem
gens, gentis	f	gens	gent	gentem
pastor, pastoris	m	pastor	pastor	pastorem
canis, canis	m/f	canis	can	canem
arbor, arboris	f	arbor	arbor	arborem
caput, capitis	n	caput	capit	caput
Caesar, Caesaris	m	Caesar	Caesar	Caesarem

B. Match the correct terms:

4 A. Noun	1. A word that is capable of asserting something
1 B. Verb	2. Words that end in s---o---x and are not marked as exceptions and are not clearly of male gender.
7 C. Accusative case	3. Use this case for the subject of the sentence or the predicate nominative.
6 D. Masculine words	4. Names a person, place, or thing.
5 E. Neuter words	5. Words that end in l---a---n---c---e---t and are not exceptions and are not clearly of male or female gender.
2 F. Feminine words	6. Words that end in er---r---or and are not marked as exceptions and are not clearly of female gender.
3 G. Nominative case	7. Use this case for direct objects.

C. Circle the subjects and predicate nominatives, double underline the verb, and underline the direct objects. Remember that predicate nominatives follow the verb "to be," and the order of the subject/predicate nominative can be switched.[10]

(verbs are boxed)

a. Bob loves football.

b. His church has a fine choir.

c. The players always play fairly.

d. Bob is a running back.

e. Bob does not throw the ball.

---

[10] Sometimes you might think you have a verb "to be" when you really just have a helping verb. For example, in the sentence, *Elizabeth is riding her bike*, "is riding' is the present tense of the verb "to ride." "Is" is not the "to be" verb here. Instead, "Elizabeth" is the subject and "bike" the direct object. You can see this because "Elizabeth" and "bike" cannot be switched: *Her bike is riding Elizabeth* is not the same thing.

D. Find the meanings for the new vocabulary. Circle the stems. Include the gender of the nouns and say whether the word is a noun or verb.

Example: a. civis, civis   Gender: <u>m/f</u>   Noun or Verb: <u>Noun</u>

           Meaning: <u>citizen</u>

b. civitas, civitatis   Gender: <u>F</u>   Noun or Verb: <u>N</u>

           Meaning: <u>state</u>

c. clamor, clamoris   Gender: <u>M</u>   Noun or Verb: <u>N</u>

           Meaning: <u>shouting, shout</u>

d. vincere   Gender: <u>X</u>   Noun or Verb: <u>V</u>

           Meaning: <u>to conquer</u>

e. virgo, virginis   Gender: <u>F</u>   Noun or Verb: <u>N</u>

           Meaning: <u>virgin</u>

f. vivere   Gender: <u>X</u>   Noun or Verb: <u>V</u>

           Meaning: <u>to live</u>

g. pastor, pastoris   Gender: <u>M</u>   Noun or Verb: <u>N</u>

           Meaning: <u>shepherd</u>

Additional Exercises:

A. This is the PRESENT chart. To fill it out remember the following: take the stem, change "e" to "i" and add the personal endings (o, s, t, mus, tis, nt). Use the word *vincere*:

The first one is done for you.

STEM: vince	Singular	Plural
1st Person	**vinco**	vincimus
2nd Person	vincis	vincitis
3rd Person	vincit	vincunt

This is the PAST chart. To fill it out remember the following: take the stem, add a "ba" to the end of it, and then add the personal endings (m, s, t, mus, tis, nt)

STEM: vince	Singular	Plural
1st Person	vincebam	vincebamus
2nd Person	vincebas	vincebatis
3rd Person	vincebat	vincebant

B. Translate into Latin.

If you are wondering how to do this, treat each verb as if it has a pronoun as a subject. That's the ending that goes on the verb. For example,

"Caesar believes."

Caesar is the subject and so would be first form: Caesar.

What pronoun would stand in place of Caesar? "He." So I translate the verb as "he believes," which is "credit." So my sentence is "Caesar credit."

a. The dog drinks.   Canis bibit.

b. He drinks.   Bibit.

c. You drink.   Bibis.

C. Translate into Latin.

a. The leader was conquering Caesar. Dux vincebat Caesarem.

b. The shepherd sends the dog.   Pastor mittit canem.

c. The leader is a tree.   Dux est arbor.

D. Translate into English:

a. Bibimus.   We drink.

b. Creditis.   You (pl) believe.

c. Vincis.   You conquer.

d. Curro.   I run.

e. Bibebamus.   We were drinking.

Lesson XI
ೋCನಿQ

Practice Exercises:

A. Make possessives out of these words:

a. girl   <u>girl's (of the girl)</u>   b. men   <u>men's (of the men)</u>

c. house   <u>house's (of the house)</u>   d. dogs   <u>dogs' (of the dogs)</u>

e. foot   <u>foot's (of the foot)</u>   f. feet   <u>feet's (of the feet)</u>

g. grass   <u>grass' (of the grass)</u>   h. goddess   <u>goddess' (of the goddess)</u>

B. Give the genitive form of all of these Latin words:

a. virtus, virtutis   <u>virtutis</u>   b. nomen, nominis   <u>nominis</u>

c. vox, vocis   <u>vocis</u>   d. veritas, veritatis   <u>veritatis</u>

e. urbs, urbis   <u>urbis</u>   f. lex, legis   <u>legis</u>

C. Underline all the nouns that possess something or someone.

a. Danny loves to eat <u>Patrick's</u> marshmallows.

b. <u>Suzie's</u> cup was situated precariously on the edge of the table.

c. <u>Mary's</u> favorite animal is a fluffy orange one.

d. Molly thinks that that old car is a piece of <u>junk.</u>

D. Here is a "copycat i---lover" word. Remember how to do these:

A verb that loves its "i" will keep it, but otherwise it copycats the ---ere verbs. It doesn't have to change the "e" to "i" for the present, because it is already an "i." However, it adds the "e" for the past and future, so it can be just like the third conjugation "ere" words, but it doesn't lose its "i."

This is the PRESENT chart. To fill it out remember the following: (o, s, t, mus, tis, nt). Use the word *venire:*

The first one is done for you.

STEM: veni	Singular	Plural
1st Person	**venio**	venimus
2nd Person	venis	venitis
3rd Person	venit	veniunt

This is the PAST chart. To fill it out remember the following: take the stem, add a "ba" to the end of it, and then add the personal endings (o, s, t, mus, tis, nt).

STEM: veni	Singular	Plural
1st Person	**veniebam**	veniebamus
2nd Person	veniebas	veniebatis
3rd Person	veniebat	veniebant

Additional Exercises:

A. Put into Latin:

a. The father's dog	patris canis
b. Caesar's shouting	Caesaris clamor
c. The citizen's state	civis civitas
d. The love of light	caritas lucis
e. The light of truth	lux veritatis

B. This is the PRESENT chart. To fill it out remember the following: take the stem, change "e" to "i" and add the personal endings (o, s, t, mus, tis, nt). Use the word *ponere:*

The first one is done for you.

STEM: pone	Singular	Plural
1st Person	**pono**	ponimus
2nd Person	ponis	ponitis
3rd Person	ponit	ponunt

This is the PAST chart. To fill it out remember the following: take the stem, add a "ba" to the end of it, and then add the personal endings (m, s, t, mus, tis, nt)

STEM: pone	Singular	Plural
1st Person	ponebam	ponebamus
2nd Person	ponebas	ponebatis
3rd Person	ponebat	ponebant

C. Punctuate the possessives correctly.

    a. Logan's friend is Chinese.

    b. The horse's face indicated he missed Maggie's carrots.

    c. Allana's sisters are in college.

D. Find the meanings for the new vocabulary. Circle the stems. Include the gender of the nouns and say whether the word is a noun or verb.

a. iter, itineris   Gender: (n)   Noun or Verb: N
    Meaning: journey

b. vulnus, vulneris   Gender: (n)   Noun or Verb: N
    Meaning: wound

c. flumen, fluminis   Gender: n   Noun or Verb: N
    Meaning: river

d. corpus, corporis   Gender: (n)   Noun or Verb: N
    Meaning: body

e. pons, pontis   Gender: (m)   Noun or Verb: N
    Meaning: bridge

f. pax, pacis   Gender: f   Noun or Verb: N
    Meaning: peace

Lesson XII
ഇൗ

Practice Exercises:

A. Do the object test on the underlined words and say whether they are direct objects or indirect objects.

1. The dog handed Sam the <u>ball</u>.	Indirect	Direct
2. Susie gave <u>Rosa</u> a hair clip.	Indirect	Direct
3. Mark sent flowers to <u>Maria</u>.	Indirect	Direct
4. The child drew his mother a <u>picture</u>.	Indirect	Direct
5. Felicity showed the <u>pagans</u> courage.	Indirect	Direct

B. Underline each noun in the following sentences and then say how it is used:

<u>Squanto</u> is a famous <u>person</u>. The <u>Pilgrims</u> needed <u>food</u>. They wanted <u>ships</u> for <u>aid</u>.[1] The <u>Pilgrims</u> were not seeing a <u>ship</u>. The <u>pilgrims'</u> <u>children</u> worry. <u>Squanto's</u> <u>friends</u> work to prepare <u>food</u> to give to the <u>pilgrims</u>. The <u>pilgrims</u> are a happy <u>people</u>.

Squanto — subject	pilgrim's — possessive
person — predicate nom	children — subject
pilgrims — subject	Squanto's — possessive
food — direct object	friends — subject
ships – direct object	food — direct object
aid — object of "for what purpose" phrase	pilgrims — indirect object
Pilgrims — subject	pilgrims — subject
ship — direct object	people — predicate nom

C. Find the indirect objects in these sentences:

a. William gave Eliza a chocolate candy.

b. Logan offered Sam his green eggs.

c. Kamber told Molly a story.

d. Allana promised her mother she would go.

e. Mary showed Kamber a braid.

---
[1] This is a "for what purpose" phrase.

D. Find the meanings for the new vocabulary. Circle the stems. Include the gender of the nouns and say whether the word is a noun or verb.

a. mons, montis   Gender:(m)   Noun or Verb: N
   Meaning: mountain

b. collis, collis   Gender:(m)   Noun or Verb: N
   Meaning: hill

c. caedes, caedis   Gender: F   Noun or Verb: N
   Meaning: slaughter

d. hostis, hostis   Gender: M   Noun or Verb: N
   Meaning: enemy

e. rex, regis   Gender: M   Noun or Verb: N
   Meaning: king

f. salus, salutis   Gender: F   Noun or Verb: N
   Meaning: safety

Additional Exercises

A. Give the dative of the following words:

a. virgo, virginis   virgini
b. iter, itineris (n)   itineri
c. vulnus, vulneris (n)   vulneri
d. flumen, fluminis   flumini
e. corpus, corporis (n)   corpori
f. pons, pontis (m)   ponti
g. mons, montis (m)   monti
h. collis, collis (m)   colli
i. caedes, caedis   caedi
j. hostis, hostis   hosti
k. rex, regis   regi
l. salus, salutis   saluti

41

B. Translate into English:

a. Caesaris pater montem cedebat. Caesar's father was yielding the mountain.
b. Sum rex. I am king.
c. Dux munit urbem virgini. The leader builds the city for the virgin.
d. Pastor canem mittit. The shepherd sends the dog.

C. Put into Latin:

e. for the father's dog cani patris
f. for Caesar's shouting clamori Caesaris
g. for the state's citizen civi civitatis
h. for the enemy's king regi hostis

D. Fourth conjugation verbs are copycat i---lovers. A verb that loves its "i" will keep it, but otherwise it copycats the ---ere verbs. It doesn't have to change the "e" to "i" for the present, because it is already an "i." However, it adds the "e" for the past and future, so it can be just like the third conjugation "ere" words, but it doesn't lose its "i."

This is the PRESENT chart. To fill it out remember the following: (o, s, t, mus, tis, nt). Use the word *munire:*

The first one is done for you.

STEM: muni	Singular	Plural
1st Person	**munio**	munimus
2nd Person	munis	munitis
3rd Person	munit	muniunt

This is the PAST chart. To fill it out remember the following: take the stem, add a "ba" to the end of it, and then add the personal endings (o, s, t, mus, tis, nt).

STEM: muni	Singular	Plural
1st Person	**muniebam**	muniebamus
2nd Person	muniebas	muniebatis
3rd Person	muniebat	muniebant

Lesson XIII
☘☙

Practice Exercises

A. Put parenthesis around each prepositional phrase and underline the object of the preposition:

a. (In the <u>garden</u>,) the flowers are growing.

b. Sam went (to the hockey <u>game</u>) (with <u>Logan</u>.)

c. Allanna is waiting (for <u>cookies</u>) (from <u>Mary</u>.)

d. Molly lives (across the <u>country</u>.)

e. Kamber went (into the candy <u>shop</u>.)

f. Eliza ran (towards the <u>beach</u>) (along <u>Susanna Dr</u>.)

g. Willy sat (on the <u>table</u>;) Danny sat (under the <u>table</u>.)

h. Maggie put two chairs (at the <u>table</u>,) "Sit (on these <u>chairs</u>,) please, so the teacher doesn't worry (about <u>you</u>.)

B. Give the case that each of the underlined words would be in if translated into Latin.

a. Every Tuesday, Miss <u>Mary</u> goes to Latin class.
<u>Nominative</u>

b. She does not bring her <u>lamb.</u>
<u>Accusative</u>

c. She doesn't bring her lamb because her parents have not given <u>Mary a lamb.</u>
Mary – <u>Dative</u>, lamb – <u>Accusative</u>

d. She tells her mother, "If I had a lamb, I would sing songs for my <u>mother</u>."
<u>Dative</u>

e. <u>Mary's</u> mother smiles.
<u>Genitive</u>

f. In the <u>morning,</u> walk to the <u>garden</u>.
<u>morning — ablative, garden — accusative</u>

g. There is a <u>lamb.</u>
<u>Nominative</u>

B. (cont)

h. The lamb of <u>Mary</u> makes her happy.
   <u>Genitive</u>

i. She sings "Mary had a little lamb" to her <u>mother</u>.
   <u>Dative</u>

j. She sings it over and over because she wants to take it to Latin <u>class</u>.
   <u>Accusative</u>

k. Her mother says to her <u>father</u>, "By what <u>month</u>, will the little lamb grow from a little <u>lamb</u> and become a big sheep?" <u>father — dative, month — ablative, lamb — ablative</u>

C. Please give the ablative of the following words:

a. virtus, virtutis   Ablative: <u>virtute</u>

b. nomen, nominis   Ablative: <u>nomine</u>

c. vox, vocis   Ablative: <u>voce</u>

d. veritas, veritatis   Ablative: <u>veritate</u>

e. urbs, urbis   Ablative: <u>urbe</u>

D. What are the three special prepositions? <u>of, for, to</u>

Translate these phrases:

a. of the tribe   <u>gentis</u>

b. for the truth   <u>veritati</u>

c. for Caesar   <u>Caesari</u>

d. in the hill   <u>in colle</u>

e. to the hill (use "ad")   <u>ad collem</u>

f. to Caesar (use dative)   <u>Caesari</u>

g. to eat   <u>edere</u>

A. Give the stem and the meaning of the new words. Circle the nominative/first form.

a. princeps. principis   Stem: princip
    Meaning: chief, leading man

b. homo, hominis   Stem: homin
    Meaning: man

c. legio, legionis   Stem: legion
    Meaning: legion

d. mater, matris   Stem: matr
    Meaning: mother

e. imperator, imperatoris   Stem: imperator
    Meaning: general, emperor

f. miles, militis   Stem: milit
    Meaning: soldier

B. Fill in this chart for "sum." Underline the personal endings.

	Singular	Plural
1st Person	sum	sumus
2nd Person	es	estis
3rd Person	est	sunt

Fill in this chart for the noun *princeps, principis*:

Nominative	princeps
Genitive	principis
Dative	principi
Accusative	principem
Ablative	principe

C. Fill in the blanks:

The subject uses the nominative case in Latin, which is the first form of the word. The predicate nominative also uses the nominative case in Latin. The accusative case is used for direct objects, as well as for objects of the preposition "toward (to)." The possessive in English is expressed by an " 's" or by the preposition "of." In Latin the possessive is called the genitive, and it is the second form of the noun. The dative case is used for objects of the preposition " for " and for objects of the preposition "to." It is also used for indirect objects. Use the accusative or ablative case for objects of all prepositions except for "of", "for" and sometimes "to."

.

D. Identify the cases of each of the following:

a.	Saluti	Nom	Gen	Dat	Acc	Abl
b.	Pacem	Nom	Gen	Dat	Acc	Abl
c.	Corporis	Nom	Gen	Dat	Acc	Abl
d.	Imperator	Nom	Gen	Dat	Acc	Abl
e.	Luce	Nom	Gen	Dat	Acc	Abl
f.	Homo	Nom	Gen	Dat	Acc	Abl

Practice Exercises

A. Looking at the plural column for neuter nouns and masculine/feminine nouns you will notice that only two endings are different. Compare these two charts.

What 2 cases have different endings? <u>The nominative and accusative are</u> <u>different. Neuter nominative and accusative are "a," and masculine/feminine</u> <u>nominative and accusative are "es."</u>

B. Make plurals out of these nouns, keeping the same case:

a. Homini	<u>hominibus</u>
b. Legione	<u>legionibus</u>
c. Salus	<u>salutes</u>
d. Corporis	<u>corporum</u>
e. Vulnus	<u>vulnera</u>
f. Urbem	<u>urbes</u>

C. Look back at the two charts you were given in the lesson. They show you what the different cases should look like with masculine/feminine words (homo, hominis) and neuter words (flumen, fluminis). Now look at the two charts below. Label these two charts correctly. Which is the <u>singular</u> chart? Which is the <u>plural</u> chart?

<u>Singular</u> CHART

Nominative = Subject = First Form
Genitive = Possessive ('s or the object of "of") = Second Form
Dative = Indirect Object (object of "for") = Stem + i
Accusative <u>MASCULINE/FEMININE</u> = Direct Object or Object of some preps. = Stem + em
Accusative <u>NEUTER</u> = Direct Object or Object of some preps. = Same as Nominative
Singular Ablative = Object of some prepositions = Stem + e

Nominative MASCULINE AND FEMININE = Subject = Stem + ES
Nominative NEUTER = Subject = Stem + A
Genitive = Possessive ('s or the object of "of") = Stem + UM
Dative = Indirect Object (object of "for") = Stem + IBUS
Accusative = Direct Object or Object of some prepositions = Same as Nominative Plural
Ablative = Object of some prepositions = Stem + IBUS

D. Fill out the charts.

These are FUTURE charts. To fill one out for a third conjugation verb remember the following: take the stem and add the endings. (The first form is an exception). The personal endings are m, s, t, mus, tis, nt.

The first one is done for you.

STEM: pete	Singular	Plural
1st Person	**petam — I will seek**	petemus — we will seek
2nd Person	petes — you will seek	petetis — you (pl) will seek
3rd Person	petet — he (she, it) will seek	petent — they will seek

To fill it out for a fourth conjugation verb remember the following: keep the "i" and copy the endings for petam above. (The first form is an exception). The personal endings are m, s, t, mus, tis, nt.

The first one is done for you.

STEM: veni	Singular	Plural
1st Person	**veniam--- I will come**	veniemus — we will come
2nd Person	venies — you will come	venietis — you (pl) will come
3rd Person	veniet — he (she, it) will come	venient — they will come

Additional Exercises

A. Build these plurals

Example word: *arbor, arboris*

1. Write down the second form of the noun:	arboris
2. Subract the –is:	–is
3. Give the stem:	arbor
4. Add the Ablative Plural ending to the stem:	arbor + ibus

a. Word: caput, capitis

Write down the second form of the noun:	capitis
Subtract the –is:	–is
Give the stem:	capit
Add the Genitive Plural ending to the stem:	capit + um

b. Word: salus, salutis

Write down the second form of the noun:	salutis
Subtract the –is:	–is
Give the stem:	salut
Add the Accusative Plural ending to the stem:	salut + es

c. Word: mons, montis

Write down the second form of the noun:	montis
Subtract the –is:	–is
Give the stem:	mont
Add the Dative Plural ending to the stem:	mont + ibus

d. Word: pastor, pastoris

Write down the second form of the noun:	pastoris
Subtract the –is:	–is
Give the stem:	pastor
Add the Ablative Plural ending to the stem:	pastor + ibus

B. Complete the chart:

Gender	Case	Singular	Plural
M/F	Nominative = Subject	1st Form	Stem + ES
N			Stem + A
All	Genitive = Possessive	2nd Form	Stem + um
All	Dative = Indirect Object	Stem + I	Stem + ibus
M/F	Accusative = Direct Object or Objects of some prepositions	Stem + EM	Same as Nom.
N		Same as Nom.	
All	Ablative = Objects of some prepositions	Stem + e	Stem + ibus

C. Translate from Latin to English:

a. Ducam Caesaris agminem.   I will lead Caesar's column.

b. Virgo bibit.   The virgin drinks.

c. Caesar dicebat gentibus.   Caesar was speaking to the tribes.

d. Audies flumen.   You will hear the river.

D. Translate from English to Latin.

a. The dog was hearing Cicero.   Canis audiebat Ciceronem.

b. The tribes will come to Caesar.   Gentes venient ad Caesarem.

c. The tribes will come for Cicero.   Gentes venient Ciceroni.

Lesson XV

ಬಿಂಬ

Practice Exercises

A. Identify and punctuate correctly all appositives in the following sentences:

a. The children, members of the choir, were all riding the bus.

b. New York, a city, is in the state, New York.

c. Stella has twin sisters, Rachel and Sarah.

d. Tasha, an FBI agent, found the perpetrator of the crime was Remi, a rabbit.

e. Nouns, a part of speech, are fun to study.

B. Underline the appositives. What case would each appositive take?

a. Albert, the famous <u>theologian</u>, started as a scientist.   nominative

b. Juliette called the dog, <u>Fido</u>.   accusative

c. Marietta, my <u>sister</u>, gave a present to Jeremiah, our <u>uncle</u>.   nominative, dative

d. The dog of my brother, <u>Robert</u>, is happy.   genitive

C. In these sentences all the underlined nouns are in the nominative case. Write above each of them their use. (i.e. subject = s, appositive = a, predicate nominative= pn)

S   A   PN

<u>Sophia</u> loves football. Matthew, her <u>brother</u>, laughs at her. Sophia is a mad <u>girl</u>.

S   A

<u>Girls</u> love sports! Maria, Sophia's <u>mom</u>, says that without spectators, spectator

PN   A

sports would die out. That is a sad <u>thought</u>. Matthew, a football <u>fan</u>, is glad that

there are many fans of the sport.

D. Give the stem and the meaning of the following words.

Circle the nominative/first form of the nouns:

a. mare, maris   Stem: mar   Meaning: sea
b. defendere   Stem: defende   Meaning: to defend
c. edere   Stem: ede   Meaning: to eat
d. gerrere   Stem: gerre   Meaning: to wage
e. fons, fontis   Stem: font   Meaning: fountain
f. dolor, doloris   Stem: dolor   Meaning: sorrow

Additional Exercises

A. Complete this chart:

Gender	Case	Singular	Plural
M/F	Nominative = Subject	1st Form	Stem + ES
N			Stem + A
All	Genitive = Possessive	**2nd Form**	**Stem + UM**
All	Dative = Indirect Object	Stem + I	STEM + IBUS
M/F	Accusative = Direct Object or Objects of some prepositions	Stem + EM	Same as Nom
N		Same as Nom	
All	Ablative = Objects of some prepositions	Stem + E	Stem + IBUS

Using these review charts, fill in the blank charts with the assigned words.

Regular Present	Copycat i---lovers Present	Regular Past	Copycat i---lovers Past
rego	audio	regebam	audiebam
regis	audis	regebas	audiebas
regit	audit	regebat	audiebat
regimus	audimus	regebamus	audiebamus
regitis	auditis	regebatis	audiebatis
regunt	audiunt	regebant	audiebant

Regular Future	Copycat i---lovers Future
regam	audiam
reges	audies
reget	audiet
regemus	audiemus
regetis	audietis
regent	audient

B. Agere:

STEM: age	Present	Past	Future
1st Singular	ago	agebam	agam
2nd Singular	agis	agebas	ages
3rd Singular	agit	agebat	aget
1st Plural	agimus	agebamus	agemus
2nd Plural	agitis	agebatis	agetis
3rd Plural	agunt	agebant	agent

C. Munire (a copycat i---lover):

STEM: muni	Present	Past	Future
1st Singular	munio	muniebam	muniam
2nd Singular	munis	muniebas	munies
3rd Singular	munit	muniebat	muniet
1st Plural	munimus	muniebamus	muniemus
2nd Plural	munitis	muniebatis	munietis
3rd Plural	muniunt	muniebant	munient

D. Translate the following sentences:

a. Fons currit de monte. The fountain runs from the mountain.

b. Caesar est rex.   Caesar is the king.

c. Rex est Caesar.   The king is Caesar.

d. Canis audiebat vocem Ciceronis The dog was hearing the voice of Cicero.

e. The man will seek the safety of the state against the enemy, Caesar.

Homo petet salutem civitatis contra hostem, Caesarem.

Lesson XVI
ഉരു

Practice Exercises

A. Are the following nouns i --- stem or regular?

a. pars, partis	I --- Stem	Regular
b. dux, ducis	I --- Stem	Regular
c. sol, solis (masculine)	I --- Stem	Regular
d. tempus, temporis (neuter)	I --- Stem	Regular
e. urbs, urbis	I --- Stem	Regular
f. caedes, caedis	I --- Stem	Regular
g. mons, montis	I --- Stem	Regular
h. collis, collis	I --- Stem	Regular

B. Decline these nouns:

	a. collis, collis	b. sol, solis	c. tempus, temporis
Nom SING	collis	sol	tempus
Gen SING	collis	solis	temporis
Dat SING	colli	soli	tempori
ACC SING	collem	solem	tempus
Abl SING	colle	sole	tempore
Nom PLUR	colles	soles	tempora
Gen PLUR	collium	solum	temporum
Dat PLUR	collibus	solibus	temporibus
Acc PLUR	colles	soles	tempora
Abl PLUR	collibus	solibus	temporibus

C. Which of the following words have ---ium in the genitive plural? Circle them.

a. mons, montis

b. virgo, virginis

c. pastor, pastoris

d. lux, lucis

e. flumen, fluminis

f. collis, collis

g. caedes, caedis

h. pars, partis

i. sol, solis

j. urbs, urbis

k. iter, itineris (n)

l. rex, regis

D. Give the stem and the meaning of the following words. Circle the nominative/first form of the nouns:

a. oratio, orationis	Stem: oration	Meaning: prayer
b. panis, panis (masc)	Stem: pan	Meaning: bread
c. sol, solis (masc)	Stem: sol	Meaning sun
d. salus, salutis	Stem: salut	Meaning: safety
e. tempus, temporis (neut)	Stem: tempor	Meaning time
f. regere	Stem: rege	Meaning: to rule
g. trahere	Stem: trahe	Meaning: to draw
h. tentatio, tentationis	Stem: tentation	Meaning: temptation
i. scribere	Stem: scribe	Meaning: to write
j. sentire	Stem: senti	Meaning: to feel
k.crux, cruces	Stem: cruc	Meaning: cross

Additional Exercises

A. Complete this chart:

Gender	Case	Singular	Plural
M/F	Nominative = Subject	1st Form	Stem + ES
N			Stem + A
All	Genitive = Possessive	**2nd Form**	**Stem + UM**
All	Dative = Indirect Object	Stem + I	Stem + IBUS
M/F	Accusative = Direct Object or Objects of some prepositions	Stem + EM	Same as Nom
N		Same as Nom	
All	Ablative = Objects of some prepositions	Stem + e	Stem + IBUS

B. Complete this chart (notice the IUM):

Gender	Case	Singular	Plural
M/F	Nominative = Subject	1st Form	Stem + ES
N			Stem + IA
All	Genitive = Possessive	**2nd Form**	**Stem + IUM**
All	Dative = Indirect Object	Stem + I	Stem + IBUS
M/F	Accusative = Direct Object or Objects of some prepositions	Stem + EM	Same as Nom
N		Same as Nom	
M/F	Ablative = Objects of some prepositions	Stem + E	Stem + IBUS
N		Stem + I	

C. Fill out this chart for the regular verb *trahere*:

STEM: trahe	Present	Past	Future
1st Singular	traho	trahebam	traham
2nd Singular	trahis	trahebas	trahes
3rd Singular	trahit	trahebat	trahet
1st Plural	trahimus	trahebamus	trahemus
2nd Plural	trahitis	trahebatis	trahetis
3rd Plural	trahunt	trahebant	trahent

Fill out this chart for the copycat i---lover word *sentire*:

STEM: senti	Present	Past	Future
1st Singular	sentio	sentiebam	sentiam
2nd Singular	sentis	sentiebas	senties
3rd Singular	sentit	sentiebat	sentiet
1st Plural	sentimus	sentiebamus	sentiemus
2nd Plural	sentitis	sentiebatis	sentietis
3rd Plural	sentiunt	sentiebant	sentient

D. Underline all the nouns in these sentences. Say what case they are/would be in Latin. Then translate the nouns. (Verbs are done for you.)

a. Caesar seeks peace for the tribes.

  Notes on cases: Caesar — nominative, peace — accusative, tribes — dative

  Translation: Caesar petit pacem gentibus.

b. The leader of the army was running to the river. (Use "agmen" for army")

  Notes on cases: leader — nominative, army — genitive, river — accusative

  Translation: Dux agminis currebat ad flumen.

c. Canis Ciceronis defendet montem duci.

  Notes on cases: Canis — nominative, Ciceronis — genitive, montem — accusative, duci — dative

  Translation: Cicero's dog will defend the mountain for the leader.

d. Sum pastor.

  Notes on cases: pastor — nominative

  Translation: I am a shepherd.

Review II & Culture Study

Practice Exercises

A. Answer the following questions:

a. Does your house have a culina? yes (a kitchen)

b. What would a Roman call your bedroom? cubiculum

c. A Roman name for a bathroom is a latrina

d. Do you have a tablinum in your house? (a study)

e. In the picture is the triclinium or summer triclinium bigger? the trincinium

Make the floor plan for your own villa. Make sure your villa has 2 tabernas, a triclinium, culina, latrina, tablinium, cubiculums, peristylium, and impluvium

B. Solve the following (use Roman numerals and names):

a. C + I = 101

b V + III = VIII

c. VIII --- V = III

d. I + IX = X

e. VI + II = VIII

f. X --- V = V

C. Write the Roman names for the following numbers:

a. III = <u>tres</u>   b. C = <u>centum</u>   c. IX = <u>novem</u>

d. X = <u>decem</u>   e. I = <u>unus</u>   f. VI = <u>sex</u>

Challenge! Based upon what you can learn from the above what numbers in English to you think these are?

XX = <u>20</u>   CXI = <u>111</u>   XXV = <u>25</u>

Additional Exercises

A. Complete this chart:

Gender	Case	Singular	Plural
M/F	**Nominative = Subject**	1st Form	Stem + ES
N			Stem + A
All	**Genitive = Possessive**	**2nd Form**	**Stem + UM**
All	**Dative = Indirect Object**	Stem + I	Stem + IBUS
M/F	**Accusative = Direct Object or Objects of some prepositions**	Stem + EM	Same as Nom
N		Same as Nom	
All	**Ablative = Objects of some prepositions**	Stem + E	Stem + IBUS

Complete this chart (notice the IUM):

Gender	Case	Singular	Plural
M/F	Nominative = Subject	1st Form	Stem + ES
N			Stem + IA
All	Genitive = Possessive	**2nd Form**	**Stem + IUM**
All	Dative = Indirect Object	Stem + I	Stem + IBUS
M/F	Accusative = Direct Object or Objects of some prepositions	Stem + EM	Same as Nom
N		Same as Nom	
M/F	Ablative = Objects of some prepositions	Stem + E	Stem + IBUS

B. Fill out this chart for the regular verb *edere:*

STEM: ede	Present	Past	Future
1st Singular	edo	edebam	edam
2nd Singular	edis	edebas	edes
3rd Singular	edit	edebat	edet
1st Plural	edimus	edebamus	edemus
2nd Plural	editis	edebatis	edetis
3rd Plural	edunt	edebant	edent

Fill out this chart for the copycat i---lover word *audire:*

STEM: audi	Present	Past	Future
1st Singular	audio	audiebam	audiam
2nd Singular	audis	audiebas	audies
3rd Singular	audit	audiebat	audiet
1st Plural	audimus	audiebamus	audiemus
2nd Plural	auditis	audiebatis	audietis
3rd Plural	audiunt	audiebant	audient

C. Write out the i---stem rules:

A noun is i – stem if it…..
1. Ends in is or es in the nominative first form and has the same number of syllables in the first and second form.
2. Ends in s or x in the nominative first form and has a stem that ends in two consonants
3. Ends in al, ar, or e in the nominative first form (neuter nouns).

D. Review your vocabulary by matching these:

f	laudare	a.	to drink
h	credere	b.	to eat
c	venire	c.	to come
j	mittere	d.	before
a	bibere	e.	into, onto
d	ante (acc)	f.	to praise
g	in (abl)	g.	in, on
e	in (acc)	h.	to believe
i	de (abl)	i.	down from
b	edere	j.	to send

e	pars, partis	a.	mountain
j	caput, capitis	b.	legion
d	mare, maris	c.	chief
a	mons, montis	d.	sea
b	legio, legionis	e.	part
c	princeps, principis	f.	slaughter
g	pons, pontis	g.	bridge

f	caedes, caedis		h. column, army
h	agmen, agminis		i. to wage
i	gerrere		j. head

e	sum		a. leader
i	agere		b. river
f	dolor, doloris		c. to put
j	post (acc)		d. fountain
c	ponere		e. I am
d	fons, fontis		f. pain, sorrow
b	flumen, fluminis		g. shout
g	clamor, clamoris		h. tree
a	dux, ducis		i. to do
h	arbor, arboris		j. after

Lesson XVII

ℰᴑℭ℞

Practice Exercises

A. Say whether each of the following is simple or compound:

a. Los Angeles and San Francisco are in California.   simple

b. Mr. Long drove to Los Angeles and sailed to Hawaii.   simple

c. I waived to Elizabeth, but she did not see me.   compound

d. His hair was curly; his face was dirty.   compound

e. Trees waved in the wind, and flowers danced as well.   compound

f. Odessa and Moscow are far---away places.   simple

B. Punctuate this correctly:

The horse and buggy is a thing of the past. Today men drive cars and some men take buses. Airplanes have replaced trains for long distance travel. Boats are still around but they are becoming obsolete quickly with the invention of the scuba car.

C. Make up two of your own compound sentences and two of your own simple sentences:

(answers my vary)

a.

_____

_____

b.

_____

_____

c.

_____

_____

d.

_____

_____

D. Say whether the underlined words are a phrase or a clause:

a. Roman schools were for boys only because <u>girls learned at home.</u> clause

b. Girls learned how <u>to run a household</u>. phrase

c. Boys learned subjects, <u>such as math.</u> phrase

d. Boys studied hard in school, and <u>they played games in school</u>. clause

Additional Exercises

A. Fill in this chart:

Number	CASE	3rd Regular Masculine/ Feminine	3rd I - stem Masculine/ Feminine	3rd Regular Neuter	3rd I – stem Neuter
Singular	Nominative	arbor	fons	tempus	mare
	Genitive	arboris	fontis	temporis	maris
	Dative	arbori	fonti	tempori	mari
	Accusative	arborem	fontem	temporem	mare
	Ablative	arbore	fonte	tempore	mari
Plural	Nominative	arbores	fontes	tempora	maria
	Genitive	arborum	fontium	temporum	marium
	Dative	arboribus	fontibus	temporibus	maribus
	Accusative	arbores	fontes	tempora	maria
	Ablative	arboribus	fontibus	temporibus	maribus

B. Fill out this chart for the regular verb *trahere*:

STEM: trahe	Present	Past	Future
1st Singular	traho	trahebam	traham
2nd Singular	trahis	trahebas	trahes
3rd Singular	trahit	trahebat	trahet
1st Plural	trahimus	trahebamus	trahemus
2nd Plural	trahitis	trahebatis	trahetis
3rd Plural	trahunt	trahebant	trahent

Fill out this chart for the copycat i---lover word *venire*:

STEM: veni	Present	Past	Future
1st Singular	venio	veniebam	veniam
2nd Singular	venis	veniebas	venies
3rd Singular	venit	veniebat	veniet
1st Plural	venimus	veniebamus	veniemus
2nd Plural	venitis	veniebatis	venietis
3rd Plural	veniunt	veniebant	venient

C. Sort these words into the correct boxes:

urbs, urbis   rex, regis   corpus, corporis

civis, civis   lux, lucis   flumen, fluminis

mare, maris   panis, panis   sol, solis

	Regular	I Stem
Masculine/Feminine	rex, regis lux, lucis sol, solis	urbs, urbis civis, civis panis, panis
Neuter	corpus, corporis flumen, fluminis	mare, maris

D. Translate:

a. Dicit orationem.   He says the prayer.

b. Gens veniet in agmine ad flumen. The tribe will come in a column to the river.

c. Fons currebat de montibus.   The fountain was running from the mountains.

Lesson XVIII

൏ഽൢ

Practice Exercises

A. Circle the interjections in the following sentences:

    a. Yikes! A bat is in our house.
    b. No! I can't believe you ate that cake.
    c. Oh! Where is my little dog?
    d. Alas! The movie had a sad ending.
    e. Hurrah! That elephant is happy.

B. Let's review the new conjunctions and interjections. Give the meanings to these words:

et <u>and</u>	vel <u>or</u>	sed <u>but</u>
O <u>Oh</u>	eheu <u>alas</u>	

C. Put into Latin the following:

a. You (pl) are. <u>estis</u>	b. He is. <u>est</u>
c. You (pl) are eating. <u>editis</u>	d. He is eating. <u>edit</u>
e. We were eating. <u>edebamus</u>	f. We were. <u>eramus</u>
g. I am eating. <u>edo</u>	h. I am. <u>sum</u>

D. In Latin every preposition, conjunction, and interjection is indeclinable. That means it has one form in Latin. In the following paragraph mark the words that would be indeclinable.

Mary was eating dinner with Hannah. Alas! The rice burned, and Hannah was unhappy. By burning the rice, Hannah felt she had ruined the dinner and Mary's appetite. "O, Mary, the rice is burned!" said Hannah. "Yea!" responded Mary. "I don't like rice but I do like fire. Let's burn it again." Hannah thought Mary was silly but nice without a doubt.

Additional Exercises

A. Fill in this chart:

Number	CASE	3rd Regular Masculine/ Feminine	3rd I – stem Masculine/ Feminine	3rd Regular Neuter	3rd I – stem Neuter
Singular	**Nominative**	rex	panis	corpus	mare
	Genitive	regis	panis	corporis	maris
	Dative	regi	pani	corpori	mari
	Accusative	regem	panem	corpus	mare
	Ablative	rege	pane	corpore	mari
Plural	**Nominative**	reges	panes	corpora	maria
	Genitive	regum	panium	corporum	marium
	Dative	regibus	panibus	corporibus	maribus
	Accusative	reges	panes	corpora	maria
	Ablative	regibus	panibus	corporibus	maribus

B. Fill out this chart for the regular verb *vincere:*

STEM: vince	Present	Past	Future
1st Singular	vinco	vincebam	vincam
2nd Singular	vincis	vincebas	vinces
3rd Singular	vincit	vincebat	vincet
1st Plural	vincimus	vincebamus	vincemus
2nd Plural	vincitis	vincebatis	vincetis
3rd Plural	vincunt	vincebant	vincent

Fill out this chart for the copycat i---lover word *audire*:

STEM: audi	Present	Past	Future
1st Singular	audio	audiebam	audiam
2nd Singular	audis	audiebas	audies
3rd Singular	audit	audiebat	audiet
1st Plural	audimus	audiebamus	audiemus
2nd Plural	auditis	audiebatis	audietis
3rd Plural	audiunt	audiebant	audient

C. Translate:

a. The rivers run to the sea.   Flumina currunt ad mare.

b. Cicero and Caesar will eat bread with the citizen.
Cicero et Caesar edent panem cum cive.

c. The enemy or the tribe was coming to the city.
Hostis vel gens veniebat ad urbem.

d. Hostes Romae Caesarem occidebant.   The enemies of Rome were killing
   Caesar.

e. Est Ciceronis canis.   It is Cicero's dog.

f. Pastoris canis regit montem gentibus.
The shepherd's dog rules the mountain for the tribes.

D. Mark the words that are I – stem and say which rule applies.

A noun is i – stem if it…..

Rule A: Ends in –is or –es in the nominative first form and has the same number of syllables in the first and second form.

Rule B: Ends in –s or –x in the nominative first form and has a stem that ends in two consonants

Rule C: Ends in –al, ---ar, or –e in the nominative first form (neuter nouns).

A. homo, hominis (m)	___ i – stem	Rule: _____	X Regular
B. urbs, urbis	X i – stem	Rule: B	__Regular
C. flumen, fluminis	___ i – stem	Rule: _____	X Regular
D. civitas, civitatis	___ i – stem	Rule: _____	X Regular
E. canis, canis (m/f)	X i – stem	Rule: A	__Regular
F. lex, legis	___ i – stem	Rule: _____	X Regular
G. gens, gentis	X i – stem	Rule: B	__Regular
H. fons, fontis (m)	X i – stem	Rule: B	__Regular
I. caedes, caedis	X i – stem	Rule: A	__Regular
J. hostis, hostis	X i – stem	Rule: A	__Regular
K. collis, collis (m)	X i – stem	Rule: A	__Regular
L. pars, partis	X i – stem	Rule: B	__Regular
M. agmen, agminis	___ i – stem	Rule: _____	X Regular
N. nomen, nominis	___ i – stem	Rule: _____	X Regular
O. corpus, corporis (n)	___ i – stem	Rule: _____	X Regular

74

Lesson XIX
ಬಗೆ

Practice Exercises

A. Circle the adverbs in these sentences. Ask yourself, "What words say when, where, how, or how much?"

a. Tomorrow, I will go.
b. Here we are.
c. Very quickly, he shut the door.
d. Gently, Lily petted the kitty.

B. What questions do these adverbs answer?

a. Here we are, very soon we will go. We will go happily if you come with us to the park.

here – where
very – how much
soon – when
happily – how

b. He easily won the race.

easily – how

c. See you later today.

later – when
today – when

C. In Latin, there are two kinds of adverbs. Some are formed from adjectives and some are not formed from other words. Here are some common adverbs.Look up their meanings:

a. nunc now   b. non not
c. saepe often   d. semper always
e. denique finally   f. ubi where
g. cur why   h. diu for a long time

D. Write a rule for forming the word "possum" in Latin. I will get you started.

Add "pos" before the letter "s" and "pot" before any other form. Use the forms of "sum."

Additional Exercises

A. Say whether each of the following is a helping verb or a verb "to be." (Hint: Remember that when you see the verb "is," "are," "am," "was," "were," "will be," etc. by itself you have the verb "to be." When this word is following by a verb word with an "ing" ending, your "is", "are", etc., verb is a helping verb.

a. I <u>was</u> calling the store.　　❑❑ Verb to be　　☒☒ Helping verb
b. I <u>was</u> happy.　　☒☒ Verb to be　　❑❑ Helping verb
c. The car <u>is</u> guzzling gas.　　❑❑ Verb to be　　☒☒ Helping verb
d. Gas <u>is</u> in the tank.　　☒☒ Verb to be　　❑❑ Helping verb
e. She <u>will be</u> calling the doctor.　　❑❑ Verb to be　　☒☒ Helping verb
f. She <u>will be</u> here.　　☒☒ Verb to be　　❑❑ Helping verb

B. Fill in this chart:

Number	CASE	3rd Regular Masculine/ Feminine	3rd I – stem Masculine/ Feminine	3rd Regular Neuter	3rd I – stem Neuter
Singular	Nominative	pax	caedes	tempus	mare
	Genitive	pacis	caedis	temporis	maris
	Dative	paci	caedi	tempori	mari
	Accusative	pacem	caedem	temporem	mare
	Ablative	pace	caede	tempore	mari
Plural	Nominative	paces	caedes	tempora	maria
	Genitive	pacum	caedium	temporum	marium
	Dative	pacibus	caedibus	temporibus	maribus
	Accusative	paces	caedes	tempores	maria
	Ablative	pacibus	caedibus	temporibus	maribus

C. Fill out this chart for the regular verb *scribere:*

STEM: scribe	Present	Past	Future
1st Singular	scribo	scribebam	scribam
2nd Singular	scribis	scribebas	scribes
3rd Singular	scribit	scribebat	scribet
1st Plural	scribimus	scribebamus	scribemus
2nd Plural	scribitis	scribebatis	scribetis
3rd Plural	scribunt	scribebant	scribent

Fill out this chart for the copycat i---lover word *venire:*

STEM: veni	Present	Past	Future
1st Singular	venio	veniebam	veniam
2nd Singular	venis	veniebas	venies
3rd Singular	venit	veniebat	veniet
1st Plural	venimus	veniebamus	veniemus
2nd Plural	venitis	veniebatis	venietis
3rd Plural	veniunt	veniebant	venient

D. Translate:

a. The shepherd was drinking from the fountain.
Pastor bibebat ab fonte.

b. Now the general kills part of the enemies' legion
Nunc imperator occidit partem legionis hostium.

c. Caesar muniet pontem trans flumen.
Caesar will build a bridge across the river.

d. Dux legionis semper cedet corpora et capita hostium civitati.
 The leader of the legion will always yield the bodies and heads of the enemies to the state.

Lesson XX

Practice Exercises

A. Circle any of the following words that belong to the new declension (don't worry about the meanings for now):

Maria, Mariae	poeta, poetae	ager, agri
puer, pueri	pecunia, pecuniae	urbs, urbis
pastor, pastoris	Donum, doni	herba, herbae
pater, patris	laus, laudis	silva, silvae

B. Fill in the chart for this first declension noun:

Case	Singular	Plural
Nominative	poeta	poetae
Genitive	poetae	poetarum
Dative	poetae	poetis
Accusative	poetam	poetas
Ablative	poeta	poetis

C. Find the meaning of these words:

a. copia, copiae — supply
b. filia, filiae — daughter
c. Gallia, Galliae — France
d. gloria, gloriae — glory
e. gratia, gratiae — grace
f. inopia, inopiae — scarcity, lack
g. Maria, Mariae — Mary
h. poeta, poetae (m) — poet
i. pecunia, pecuniae — money
j. nauta, nautae (m) — sailor

D. Give the correct forms:

a. *Poet* in the genitive plural   poetarum

b. *Glory* in the dative plural   gloriis

c. *Money* in the dative singular pecuniae

d. *France* in the ablative singular Gallia

e. *Mary* in the ablative plural   Mariis

f. *Supply* in the nominative plural copiae

Additional Exercises

A. Let's review the verb "to be" and the helping verb. Remember when you see the verb "is," "are," "am," "was," "were," "will be," "be," "was being" etc. by itself you have the verb "to be." When this word is following by a verb word with an "ing" ending, your "is," "are," etc. verb is a helping verb.

(answers may vary)

a. A sentence using the word "is" as a helping verb.

_____
_____

b. A sentence using the word "was" as a helping verb.

_____
_____

c. A sentence using the words "will be" as the verb "to be".

_____
_____

d. A sentence using the word "was" as the verb "to be."

_____
_____

B. Fill in this chart:

Number	CASE	3rd Regular Masculine/Feminine	3rd I – stem Masculine/Feminine	3rd Regular Neuter	3rd I – stem Neuter
Singular	Nominative	lex	pars	vulnus	mare
	Genitive	legis	partis	vulneris	maris
	Dative	legi	parti	vulneri	mari
	Accusative	legem	partem	vulnus	mare
	Ablative	lege	parte	vulnere	mari
Plural	Nominative	leges	partes	vulnera	maria
	Genitive	legum	partium	vulnerum	marium
	Dative	legibus	partibus	vulneribus	maribus
	Accusative	leges	partes	vulnera	maria
	Ablative	legibus	partibus	vulneribus	maribus

C. Fill out this chart for the irregular verb *sum*:

	Present	Past	Future
1st Singular	sum	eram	ero
2nd Singular	es	eras	eris
3rd Singular	est	erat	erit
1st Plural	sumus	eramus	erimus
2nd Plural	estis	eratis	eritis
3rd Plural	sunt	erant	erunt

Fill out this chart for the irregular word *possum:*

	Present	Past	Future
1st Singular	possum	poteram	potero
2nd Singular	potes	poteras	poteris
3rd Singular	potest	poterat	poterit
1st Plural	possumus	poteramus	poterimus
2nd Plural	potestis	poteratis	poteritis
3rd Plural	possunt	poterant	poterunt

D. Translate:

a. The column was defending the king in France.

Agmen defendebat regem in Gallia.

b. Maria (Mary) is the daughter.

Maria est filia.

c. Possumus edere panem.

We are able to eat bread.

d. Inopia montium in Gallia est dolor.

The scarcity of mountains in France is a sorrow.

Lesson XXI
ಬಿಂಗ

Practice Exercises

A. Conjugate "venire" and "credere" in the future possible. (Remember that copycat i---lovers love their "i"s!)

	credere	venire
1st Sing	credam	veniam
2nd Sing	credas	venias
3rd Sing	credat	veniat
1st Plural	credamus	veniamus
2nd Plural	credatis	veniatis
3rd Plural	credant	veniant

B. Translate:

a. Write (plural).   Scribite.
b. Run (singular).   Curre.
c. Eat (singular).   Ede.
d. Eat (plural).   Edite.
e. Conquer (singular)   Veni.
f. Live (plural)   Vivite.

C. Say what mood each of the following belongs to.

Wish = Subjunctive; Command = Imperative; Statement of Fact = Indicative

a. I call.   ○ Indicative   ○ Imperative   ○ Subjunctive
b. I will call.   ○ Indicative   ○ Imperative   ○ Subjunctive
c. May he call.   ○ Indicative   ○ Imperative   ○ Subjunctive
d. Call me.   ○ Indicative   ○ Imperative   ○ Subjunctive
e. Call today.   ○ Indicative   ○ Imperative   ○ Subjunctive
f. I may come.   ○ Indicative   ○ Imperative   ○ Subjunctive
g. We were.   ○ Indicative   ○ Imperative   ○ Subjunctive

D. Fill in the charts for this first declension noun:

Case	Singular	Plural
Nominative	gratia	gratiae
Genitive	gratiae	gratiarum
Dative	gratiae	gratiis
Accusative	gratiam	gratias
Ablative	gratia	gratiis

Additional Exercises:

A. Please do a synopsis for the following verbs.

To list the forms of a verb in each tense but in only one person and number is called to synopsize. So, for example, here is a synopsis of 'regere' in the second person, singular:

Present: regis   Past: regebas   Future: reges   Future Possible: regas

Do you see that each of these has the ending for the second person singular?

a. venire in the 2nd person plural

Present: venitis	Past: veniebatis

Future: venietis	Future Poss: veniatis

b. currere in the 1st person plural

Present: currimus	Past: currebamus
Future: curremus	Future Poss: curramus

c. edere in the 3rd person singular

Present: edit	Past: edebat
Future: edet	Future Poss: edat

B. Give the correct forms:

a. *Tree* in the genitive plural   arborum
b. *Glory* in the ablative plural   gloriis
c. *Bread* in the dative singular   pani
d. *Caesar* in the ablative singular Caesare
e. *Grace* in the genitive plural   gratiarum
f. *Horseman* in the accusative plural equites

C. Fill in this chart:

Number	CASE	3rd Regular Masculine/ Feminine	3rd I – stem Masculine/ Feminine	3rd Regular Neuter	3rd I – stem Neuter
Singular	Nominative	arbor	gens	caput	mare
	Genitive	arboris	gentis	capitis	maris
	Dative	arbori	genti	capiti	mari
	Accusative	arborem	gentem	capitem	mare
	Ablative	arbore	gente	capite	mari
Plural	Nominative	arbores	gentes	capita	maria
	Genitive	arborum	gentium	capitum	marium
	Dative	arboribus	gentibus	capitibus	maribus
	Accusative	arbores	gentes	capita	maria
	Ablative	arboribus	gentibus	capitibus	maribus

B. Circle all nouns in the following and write the abbreviation for the case they would be in, in Latin, above them. (N = Nominative; G = Genitive; D = Dative; A = Accusative; Ab = Ablative)

     N   A

a. Mary wants to eat apples today.

     N   A   G   Ab

b. Sam likes the apples from the farmer's house.

     N   A   D

c. Joe saves a bag for dad.

        Ab   N   A

d. In the bag, the horses find tasty apples.

       N   A

e. Our dog likes apples too.

       N   A

f. The cat seems to fear the apples.

             N   A   G

g. Fortunately, the apples do not fear the cats of our house.

Lesson XXII
ॐ

Practice Exercises

A. Using the chart above to help you out, circle the correct pronouns:

a. (He, him) and (I, me) are working late tomorrow.
b. The teacher sent (me, I) to (his, him) car to get the chalk.
c. (We, Us) girls had loads of fun yesterday.
d. With you and (he, him) to help, (we, us) will have an easy time of it.
e. Among (we, us), (we, us) were able to eat the cake.

B. Give the person, number and Latin case for each of the following pronouns:

a. **We** are having a party.   1st person, plural, nominative
b. I want **you**, John, to go.   2nd person, singular, accusative
c. Mars has **its** own life forms.   3rd person, singular, genitive
d. I called **her**.   3rd person, singular, accusative
e. The cat sat on **me.**   1st person, singular, ablative
f. **I** doubt that.   1st person, singular, nominative
g. **Their** story is strange.   3rd person, plural, genitive
h. I want **our** brother to come.   1st person, plural, genitive

C. Underline all the pronouns in this story:

A man and <u>his</u> wife are driving along a country road. Suddenly <u>she</u> says, "<u>I</u> need to make a phone call!" <u>He</u> stops the car and turns toward <u>her</u>. "<u>You</u> will have to walk back to make the call," <u>he</u> says. A sign is nearby. <u>It</u> reads, "30 miles to nearest town." <u>She</u> doesn't seem to mind, though. <u>She</u> gets out of the car with a smile. <u>He</u> gives <u>her</u> a smile and waits in the car. <u>She</u> is back in <u>it</u> in a flash. <u>Their</u> home is a trailer!

D. Choose the correct form of the interrogative pronoun:

a. I shall invite (who, whom)?

b. (who, whom) shall I invite?

c. You have visited (who, whom)?

d. (Who, whom) have you visited?

e. It is (who, whom)?

f) (Who, Whom) is it?

Additional Exercises

A. Translate the underlined words into Latin.

a. Nero had a great love <u>of himself</u>.   sui

b. The girl got cake <u>for herself.</u>   sibi

c. Caesar wrote a book <u>about himself.</u>   de se

d. Cicero hurt <u>himself</u> with a staple gun.   se

e. The people thanked <u>themselves.</u>   se

f. She went to the town <u>herself</u>.   se

B. Fill in this chart using the verb _munire_:

(Remember: A verb that loves its "I" will keep it, but otherwise it copycats the --ere verbs. It doesn't have to change the "e" to "i" for the present, because it is already an "i". However, it adds the "e" for the past, future and future possible, so it can be just like the third conjugation ---ere words, but it doesn't lose its "i".)

STEM: muni	Present	Past	Future Regulars	Subjunctive Present (aka Future Possible)
1st Singular	munio	muniebam	muniam	muniam
2nd Singular	munis	muniebas	munies	munias
3rd Singular	munit	muniebat	muniet	muniat
1st Plural	munimus	muniebamus	muniemus	muniamus
2nd Plural	munitis	muniebatis	munietis	muniatis
3rd Plural	muniunt	muniebant	munient	muniant

C. Fully decline the following nouns:

a. pastor	b. corpus	c. fons
pastoris	corporis	fontis
pastori	corpori	fonti
pastorem	corpus	fontem
pastore	corpore	fonte
pastores	corpora	fontes
pastorum	corporum	fontium
pastoribus	corporibus	fontibus
pastores	corpora	fontes
pastoribus	corporibus	fontibus

d. nauta	e. mare	f. pars
nautae	maris	partis
nautae	mari	parti
nautam	mare	partem
nauta	mari	parte
nautae	maria	partes
<u>nautarum</u>	<u>marium</u>	<u>partium</u>
nautis	maribus	partibus
nautas	maria	partes
nautis	maribus	partibus

D. Translate:

a. Caesar was building a fountain for himself.

  Caesar muniebat fontem sibi.

b. The sailor seeks the slaughter of the tribes' leader.

  Nauta petit caedem gentium/gentis ducis.

c. Vincamus per crucem cum Maria.

  May we conquer through the cross with Mary.

d. Pete panem ante inopiam pecuniae.

  Seek bread before a scarcity of money.

Lesson XXIII

ಬಿಐಆ

Practice Exercises

A. Give the correct forms:

a. *Boy* in the genitive plural   puerorum

b. *Gift* in the accusative singular donum

c. *Field* in the ablative plural   agris

d. *Slave* in the dative singular   servo

e. *Boy* in the genitive singular   pueri

f. *Field* in the dative plural   agris

B. Look up the meanings of these words:

a. amicus, amici   friend
b. bellum, belli   war
c. caelum, caeli   heaven
d. Christus, Christi   Christ
e. Christianus, Christiani Christian
f. Deus, Dei   God
g. dominus, domini   lord
h. filia, filiae   daughter
i. filius, filii   son
j. frumentum, frumenti   grain
k. Gallus, Galli   a Frenchman
l. gladius, gladii   sword
m. imperium, imperii   command, power, empire
n. mundus, mundi   world
o. murus, muri   wall
p. numerus, numeri   number
q. praemium, praemii   reward
r. periculum, periculi   danger
s. populus, populi   people

C. Fill in the chart with the first declension word *poeta, poetae*:

Case	Singular	Plural
Nominative	poeta	poetae
Genitive	poetae	poetarum
Dative	poetae	poetis
Accusative	poetam	poetas
Ablative	poeta	poetis

Fill in the chart with the second declension word *servus, servi:*

Case	Singular	Plural
Nominative	servus	servi
Genitive	servi	servorum
Dative	servo	servis
Accusative	servum	servos
Ablative	servo	servis

Fill in the chart with the second declension word *donum, doni*:

Case	Singular	Plural
Nominative	donum	dona
Genitive	doni	donorum
Dative	dono	donis
Accusative	donum	dona
Ablative	dono	donis

D. Give the gender & declension of these words:

a. dolor, doloris	Gender: m	Dec: 3
b. nauta, nautae	Gender: m	Dec: 1
c. panis, panis (m)	Gender: m	Dec: 3
d. donum, doni	Gender: n	Dec: 2
e. mons, montis (m)	Gender: m	Dec: 3
f. servus, servi	Gender: m	Dec: 2
g. gloria, gloriae	Gender: f	Dec: 1
h. crux, crucis	Gender: f	Dec: 3
i. vox, vocis	Gender: f	Dec: 3
j. filius, flii	Gender: m	Dec: 2
k. pons, pontis (m)	Gender: m	Dec: 3
l. puer, pueri	Gender: m	Dec: 2
m. ager, agri	Gender: m	Dec: 2
n. poeta, poetae (m)	Gender: m	Dec: 1
o. gratia, gratiae	Gender: f	Dec: 1
p. eques, equitis (m)	Gender: m	Dec: 3
q. tentatio, tentationis	Gender: f	Dec: 3

Additional Exercises

A. Circle all the pronouns in this passage.

"Who is it?" asked Timothy.

"It is us," said a strange

voice.

"Us! Oh, please. It is one person and it is my sister."

"What made you guess it was me?" asked the voice.

"The guess was just luck, but the "me" made me sure!" laughed Timothy. "If you

don't want me to guess, don't use your pronouns

correctly."

B. Fill in this chart using the verb _munire_:

(Remember: A verb that loves its "I" will keep it, but otherwise it copycats the --ere verbs. It doesn't have to change the "e" to "i" for the present, because it is already an "i". However, it adds the "e" for the past, future and future possible, so it can be just like the third conjugation ---ere words, but it doesn't lose its "i".)

STEM: cede	Present	Past	Future Regulars	Subjunctive Present (aka Future Possible)
1st Singular	cedo	cedebam	cedam	cedam
2nd Singular	cedis	cedebas	cedes	cedas
3rd Singular	cedit	cedebat	cedet	cedat
1st Plural	cedimus	cedebamus	cedemus	cedamus
2nd Plural	ceditis	cedebatis	cedetis	cedatis
3rd Plural	cedunt	cedebant	cedent	cedant

C. They are missing capitals. Underline or circle the letters that should be capital. Add in periods and apostrophes where needed.

i went to a great party at maggie's house. there were many animals at the party. i can't say how many. my favorite was danny's horse. maggie loves the horse and so danny gave it to her. he misses it but dr. phil told him he would feel good inside for giving her his horse. maggie is so much happier to have danny's horse than danny's flowers. she wrote a letter to danny to thank him and sent it thurs. to his house in pennsylvania.

95

D. Follow directions below.

(answers may vary)

a. Write your own sentence that has a contraction in it, a possessive in it, and a period and capital of course!

_____

_____

b. Write your own sentence that has an abbreviation in it, a contraction in it, and a period and capital, of course.

_____

_____

c. Write your own sentence that has a plural possessive and a singular possessive in it, as well as a period and capital.

_____

_____

d. Write your own sentence that has proper name, a proper place name and a contraction in it, as well as a period and a capital.

_____

_____

Lesson XXIV

ଞଓର

Practice Exercises

A. Underline all adjectives in this paragraph:

Across the <u>sparkling azure ocean</u> waters danced the <u>delightful</u> dolphins. <u>Smiling</u> faces appeared from the <u>white</u> foam as the <u>frolicsome</u> creatures rose out of the <u>deep blue</u> depths. They made a <u>smooth</u>, <u>effortless</u> transition from the <u>thin</u> air to the <u>rolling</u> waves below. Their <u>strong</u> bodies and <u>erect</u> fins made them appear as the <u>proud</u> owners of the <u>seven</u> seas.

B. Circle the adjectives that are not followed by nouns in these sentences:

a. The man is <u>tall</u>.   b. The <u>brave</u> die nobly.

c. The map is <u>interesting</u>.   d. The dog is <u>brave</u>.

C. List ten of your favorite adjectives and use them in sentences:

(answers may vary)

_____   _____   _____

_____   _____   _____

_____   _____   _____

_____   _____   _____

Sentences:

D. Look up the meanings of these words:

a. regnum, regni   kingdom
b. Roma, Romae   Rome
c. Romanus, Romani   a Roman
d. signum, signi   sign, standard
e. silva, silvae   forest
f. terra, terrae   land, earth
g. via, viae   road, way
h. victoria, victoriae   victory

Additional Exercises

A. Fill in the boxes with the correct words:

Nominative, Genitive, Dative, Accusative, Ablative

English Name	Latin Case Name
Subject	nominative
Predicate Nominatives	nominative
Indirect Objects/obj of "for"	dative
Direct Object	accusative
Possessives/obj of "of"	genitive
Objects of prepositions of motion (to, across, etc)	accusative
Objects of other prepositions	ablative

B. Fill out the chart:

Number	CASE	3rd Regular Masculine/ Feminine	3rd I – stem Masculine/ Feminine	3rd Regular Neuter	3rd I –stem Neuter
Singular	Nominative Genitive Dative Accusative Ablative	veritas veritatis veritati veritatem veritate	civis civis civi civem cive	iter itineris itineri iter itinere	mare maris mari mare mari
Plural	Nominative Genitive Dative Accusative Ablative	veritates veritatum veritatibus veritates veritatbus	cives civium civibus cives civibus	itinera itinerum itineribus itinera itineribus	maria marium maribus maria maribus

C. Fill in these charts. Use the verb *venire*:
(Remember: A verb that loves its "i" will keep it, but otherwise it copycats the ---ere verbs. It doesn't have to change the "e" to "i" for the present, because it is already an "i". However, it adds the "e" for the past and future, so it can be just like the third conjugation "ere" words, but it doesn't lose its "it".)

STEM: veni	Present	Past	Future Regulars	Subjunctive Present (aka Future Possible)
1st Singular	venio	veniebam	veniam	veniam
2nd Singular	venis	veniebas	venies	venias
3rd Singular	venit	veniebat	veniet	veniat
1st Plural	venimus	veniebamus	veniemus	veniamus
2nd Plural	venitis	veniebatis	venietis	veniatis
3rd Plural	veniunt	veniebant	venient	veniant

D. Compose in Latin.

(answers may vary)

a. Write a sentence that has a past verb, a subject and a direct object.

_____

_____

b. Write a sentence that has a command in it.

_____

_____

c. Write a sentence that has a form of the verb "to be" as well as a possessive (genitive).

_____

_____

Review III & Culture Study

ᔕᖇ

Practice Exercises

A. Do the math.

(Remember: 1 sestertius = 2 1/2 as   1 denarius = 10 as   1 aureus = 100 sestertius)

a. You have 12 sestertius. How many asses does this equal? <u>30 as</u>

b. Is 10 denarius more or less than 1 aureus? <u>less</u>

c. Willy has 25 denarius, 40 sestertius and 1 aureus. How much money is that in asses? <u>600 as</u>

B. Answer the question:

Allanna went to the market and found the most beautiful scarf. It was made of the finest, softest silk and dyed a beautiful purple.

"How much is it?" she asked the merchant.

"5 denarii," he replied.

"I don't have denarii, but I do have 15 sestertii."

"Sold!" said the merchant and he grabbed her 15 sesterii and handed her the scarf.

Did Allanna have to pay more or less than the quoted price of 5 denarii? <u>less</u>

C. Write out the full number:

Examples: $\overline{1} = 1000$ & $\overline{X} = \overline{10} = 10,000$

a. $\overline{100}$ = <u>100,000</u>

b. $\overline{V}$ = <u>5,000</u>

c. $\overline{7}$ = <u>7,000</u>

d. $\overline{IX}$ = <u>9,000</u>

e. $\overline{VIII}$ = <u>800,000</u>

f. $\overline{25}$ =<u>2,500,000</u>

D. Solve:

You have 1 aureus. You owe your brother 4 denarii. You owe your mother 10 denarii. You bought a toga for 15 asses. How much money do you have left in asses? (hint: figure out how many asses 1 aureus is. How many asses 1 denarius is.) 95 asses

Additional Exercises

A. Fill in this chart:

Number	CASE	3rd Regular Masculine/ Feminine	3rd I - stem Masculine/ Feminine	3rd Regular Neuter	3rd I - stem Neuter
Singular	Nominative	**crux**	**fons**	**nomen**	**mare**
	Genitive	**cruces**	**fontis**	**nominis**	**maris**
	Dative	cruci	fonti	nomini	mari
	Accusative	cruem	fontem	nomen	mare
	Ablative	cruce	fonte	nomine	mari
Plural	Nominative	cruces	fontes	nomina	maria
	Genitive	crucum	fontium	nominum	marium
	Dative	crucibus	fontibus	nominibus	maribus
	Accusative	cruces	fontes	nomina	maria
	Ablative	crucibus	fontibus	nominibus	maribus

B. Fill in these charts. Use the verb *bibere*:

STEM: bibe	Present	Past	Future Regulars	Subjunctive Present (aka Future Possible)
1st Singular	bibo	bibebam	bibam	bibam
2nd Singular	bibis	bibebas	bibes	bibas
3rd Singular	bibit	bibebat	bibet	bibat
1st Plural	bibimus	bibebamus	bibemus	bibamus
2nd Plural	bibitis	bibebatis	bibetis	bibatis
3rd Plural	bibunt	bibebant	bibent	bibant

C. Fill in the chart for the first declension word *gratia, gratiae*:

Case	Singular	Plural
Nominative	gratia	gratiae
Genitive	gratiae	gratiarum
Dative	gratiae	gratiis
Accusative	gratiam	gratias
Ablative	gratia	gratiis

Fill in the chart for the second declension word *dominus, domini*:

Case	Singular	Plural
Nominative	dominus	domini
Genitive	domini	dominorum
Dative	domino	dominis
Accusative	dominum	dominos
Ablative	domino	dominis

Fill in the chart for the second declension word *periculum, periculi*:

Case	Singular	Plural
Nominative	periculum	pericula
Genitive	periculi	periculorum
Dative	periculo	periculis
Accusative	periculum	pericula
Ablative	periculo	periculis

D. Translate:

a. There are horsemen for Caesar. (There are = they are)
Sunt equites Caesari.
b. Christ was sending friends and they were speaking truth.
Christus mittebat amicos et dicebant veritatem.
c. The shepherds will run to the river often. Pastores current ad flumen saepe.
d. The land will yield grain for the city in France.
Terra cedet frumentum urbi in Gallia.

Lesson XXV
ഇര

Practice Exercises

A. Complete the chart for the I -- stem noun *canis, canis:*

Gender	Case	Singular	Plural
M/F	Nominative = Subject	canis	canes
All	Genitive = Possessive	canis	can(i)um
All	Dative = Indirect Object	cani	canibus
M/F	Accusative = Direct Object or Objects of some prepositions	canem	canes
M/F	Ablative = Objects of some prepositions	cane	canibus

Complete the chart for the adjective *difficilis, difficile:*

Gender	Case	Singular	Plural
M/F	Nominative = Subject	difficilis	difficiles
N		difficile	difficilia
All	Genitive = Possessive	difficilis	difficilium
All	Dative = Indirect Object	difficili	difficilibus
M/F	Accusative = Direct Object or Objects of some prepositions	difficilem	difficiles
N		difficile	difficilia
All	Ablative = Objects of some prepositions	difficili	difficilibus

Match up the masculine endings for "difficilis" with "canis". They are the same
in gender, number and case, but are they the same?

Case	Singular	Plural
Nominative = **Subject**	difficilis canis	difficiles canes
Genitive = **Possessive**	difficilis canis	difficilium canum
Dative = Indirect **Object/Objects** **of "for"**	difficili cani	difficilibus canibus
Accusative = **Direct Object or** **Objects of some** **prepositions**	difficilem canem	difficiles canes
Ablative = **Objects of some** **prepositions**	difficili cane	difficilibus canibus

B. Put these phrases into Latin (all are singular):

a. Use the accusative case: bitter dog   acrem canem

b. Use the dative case: huge tree   ingenti arbori

c. Use the genitive case: difficult river   difficilis fluminis

C. Decline *bonus, boni/bona,bonae/bonum, boni*:

	Masculine	Feminine	Neuter
Nominative Sing.	bonus	bona	bonum
Genitive Sing.	boni	bonae	boni
Dative Sing.	bono	bonae	bono
Accusative Sing.	bonum	bonam	bonum
Ablative Sing.	bono	bona	bono
Nominative Plur.	boni	bonae	bona
Genitive Plur.	bonorum	bonarum	bonorum
Dative Plur.	bonis	bonis	bonis
Accusative Plur.	bonos	bonas	bona
Ablative Plur.	bonis	bonis	bonis

Decline *puella, puellae*:

Case	Singular	Plural
Nominative	puella	puellae
Genitive	puellae	puellarum
Dative	puellae	puellis
Accusative	puellam	puellas
Ablative	puella	puellis

Match up the feminine endings for "bona" with "puella". They are the same in gender, number and case, but are they the same?

Case	Singular	Plural
Nominative = Subject	bona puella	bonae puellae
Genitive = Possessive	bonae puellae	bonarum puellarum
Dative = Direct Object or Objects of some prepositions	bonae puellae	bonis puellis
Accusative = Direct Object or Objects of some prepositions	bonam puellam	bonas puellas
Ablative = Objects of some prepositions	bona puella	bonis puellis

D. Fill in the chart with the words *great man*: (Remember 'great' and 'man' are different declensions, but need to be same gender.)

Case	Singular	Plural
Nominative	magnus homo	magni homines
Genitive	magni hominis	magnorum hominum
Dative	magno homini	magnis hominibus
Accusative	magnum hominem	magnos homines
Ablative	magno homine	mangis hominibus

Additional Exercises

A. Give the correct forms of magnus,---i/magna,---ae/magnum, ---i for each of these words. Remember the correct form means the same gender, number and case. Sometimes you will also have to give the correct form of the noun as well.

a. dative, singular   magnae puellae

b. nominative, plural   magnae arbores

c. ablative, singular   magno dolore

d. accusative, singular   magnum regem

e. dative, plural   magnis montibus

f. genitive, singular   magni servi

g. nominative, singular   magnum donum

h. ablative, plural   magnis poetis

B. Put a smiley face next to the words that actually agree in gender, number and case.

a. _____ difficillia nomen

b. ☺☺ sancta caela

c. ☺☺ forti pastore

d. ☺☺ ingens periculum

e. ☺☺ longo itinere

f. _____ acris herbis

g. ☺☺ ingentem gratiam

h. ☺☺ difficili victoria

C. Translate the following sentences from English to Latin:

1. Seek heaven and great grace.
   Pete caelum et magnam gratiam.

2. The brave shepherds were building the huge city for Mary.
   Fortes pastores muniebant ingentem urbem Mariae.

3. The king will conquer the enemy across the sea.
   Rex vincent hostem trans mare.

D. Translate from Latin to English.

a. Petas pacem.
   May you seek peace.

b. Pete pacem.
   Seek peace.

c. Petis pacem.
   You are seeking peace.

d. Sancta Maria est amicus Christianorum.
   Holy Mary is a friend of Christians.

e. Christus gerebat bellum contra malos.
   Christ was waging war against the bad.

Lesson XXVI
ဢⓒ෬

Practice Exercises

A. Translate and then rearrange the word order:

a. The evil poet will seek the slaughter of the soldier.
Poeta malus caedem militis petet.

b. Will the evil poet seek the slaughter of the soldier?
Petetne poeta malus caedem militis?

c. The river runs down the mountain.
Flumen de monte currit.

d. We are not from the city.
Sumus non ab urbe.

e. We are from France.
Sumus ab Gallia.

B. Translate the following. Remember now that magnus can mean great or large/fat:

a. Magnus canis est saepe in silva.
The large/fat dog is often in the forest.
b. Montes magni caelum regunt.
The great mountains rule the sky.

C. Here are all the adjectives you learned last week. Please number them based upon what box you would put them in:

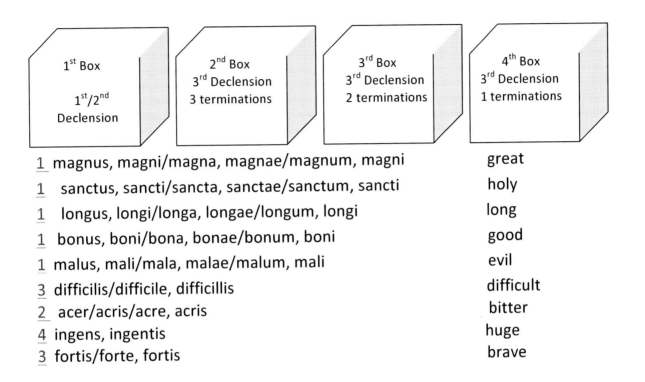

1st Box	2nd Box	3rd Box	4th Box
1st/2nd Declension	3rd Declension 3 terminations	3rd Declension 2 terminations	3rd Declension 1 terminations

<u>1</u> magnus, magni/magna, magnae/magnum, magni   great

<u>1</u> sanctus, sancti/sancta, sanctae/sanctum, sancti   holy

<u>1</u> longus, longi/longa, longae/longum, longi   long

<u>1</u> bonus, boni/bona, bonae/bonum, boni   good

<u>1</u> malus, mali/mala, malae/malum, mali   evil

<u>3</u> difficilis/difficile, difficillis   difficult

<u>2</u> acer/acris/acre, acris   bitter

<u>4</u> ingens, ingentis   huge

<u>3</u> fortis/forte, fortis   brave

D. Complete the chart for the adjective *ingens, ingentis*:

Gender	Case	Singular	Plural
M/F	Nominative = Subject	ingens	ingentes
N		ingens	ingentia
All	Genitive = Possessive	ingentis	ingentium
All	Dative = Indirect Object	ingenti	ingentibus
M/F	Accusative = Direct Object or Objects of some prepositions	ingentem	ingentes
N		ingens	ingentia
All	Ablative = Objects of some prepositions	ingenti	ingentibus

Decline *sanctus, sancti/sancta, sanctae/sanctum, sancti*:

	Masculine	Feminine	Neuter
Nominative Sing.	sanctus	sancta	sanctum
Genitive Sing.	sancti	sanctae	sancti
Dative Sing.	sancto	sanctae	sancto
Accusative Sing.	sanctum	sanctam	sanctum
Ablative Sing.	sancto	sancta	sancto
Nominative Plur.	sancti	sanctae	sancta
Genitive Plur.	sanctorum	sanctarum	sanctorum
Dative Plur.	sanctis	sanctis	sanctis
Accusative Plur.	sanctos	sanctas	sancta
Ablative Plur.	sanctis	sanctis	sanctis

Additional Exercises

A. Match up the feminine endings for "sancta" with "virgo." They are the same in gender, number and case, but are they the same?

Case	Singular	Plural
Nominative = Subject	sancta virgo	sanctae virgines
Genitive = Possessive	sanctae virginis	sanctorum virginum
Dative = Indirect Object/Objects of "for"	sanctae virgini	sanctis virginibus
Accusative = Direct Object or Objects of some prepositions	sanctam virginem	sanctas virgines
Ablative = Objects of some prepositions	sancta virgine	sanctis virginibus

B. Match each adjective with a noun it can agree with in gender, number and case.

b difficile   a. herba

c, e ingentem   b. donum

d sanctas   c. hominem

b, c malum   d. virgines

a acris   e. lucem

C. Give the second person singular ending for the following verbs in all tenses:

a. mittere

Present	Past	Future	Subjunctive/Future Possible
mittis	mittebas	mittes	mittas

b. regere

Present	Past	Future	Subjunctive/Future Possible
regis	regebas	reges	regas

c. munire

Present	Past	Future	Subjunctive/Future Possible
munis	muniebas	munies	munias

D. Put a smiley face next to the words that actually agree in gender, number and case:

a. ☺☺ bono cani   b. ☺☺ longum tempus
c. ☺☺ magnus puer   d. ___ bonum fluminum
e. ☺☺ fortium pastorum   f. ☺☺ ingens gratia
g.☺☺ ingentem gratiam   h. ____ forte victoriae

Final Review of English Grammar
ಋೋಲ

Total points 96 + 4 bonus points = 100   Student Score:

___/ 15 pts (3 per sentence) **A. Underline the simple subject once and the simple predicate twice in each of the following sentences. Circle the direct object. (Review Lessons I, II, and IX if you have questions.)**

(simple   predicates   are boxed)

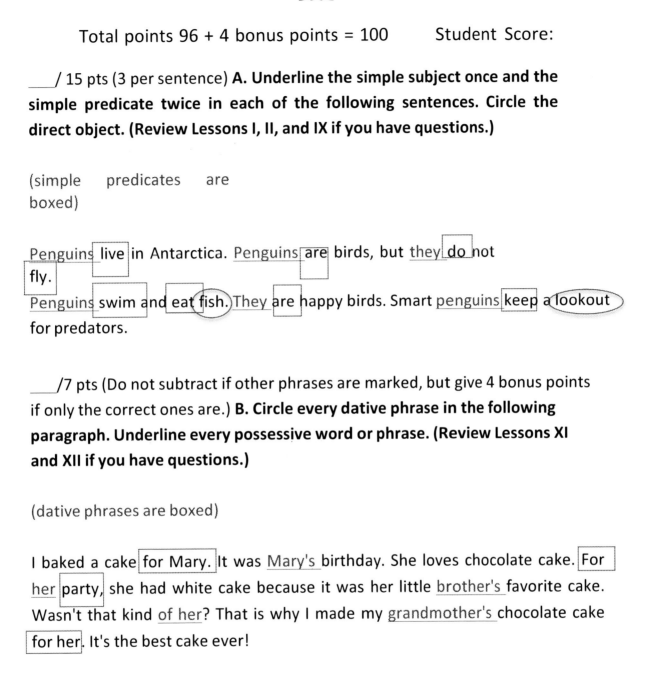

Penguins live in Antarctica. Penguins are birds, but they do not fly.
Penguins swim and eat fish. They are happy birds. Smart penguins keep a lookout for predators.

___/7 pts (Do not subtract if other phrases are marked, but give 4 bonus points if only the correct ones are.) **B. Circle every dative phrase in the following paragraph. Underline every possessive word or phrase. (Review Lessons XI and XII if you have questions.)**

(dative phrases are boxed)

I baked a cake for Mary. It was Mary's birthday. She loves chocolate cake. For her party, she had white cake because it was her little brother's favorite cake. Wasn't that kind of her? That is why I made my grandmother's chocolate cake for her. It's the best cake ever!

___/4 pts **C. Fill in the blanks with words that are adverbs. Only use one word in a blank. Adverbs tell *how*, *how much*, *when* or *where*. (Review Lesson XIX if you have questions.)**

(answers may vary)

a. I work (so, very) often. (how much)   b. I work (quickly, hard) (how)
c. I work (here, there). (where)   d. I worked (yesterday, today). (when)

___/12 pts (points for not marking "so," "are," and "when," as prepositions.)
D. Underline all prepositional phrases. However, if the phrase is a dative phrase (for) or a genitive phrase (of) or an infinitive (to + verb) cross it out. (Review Lessons VI, XI, XII, and XV if you have questions.)

By the light ~~of the silvery moon~~, I saw an owl in a tree swoop to the ground.
The owl caught a mouse when he came down from that tree.
He swooped across the land so quietly. He caught the mouse with ease ~~for a big bird~~. Owls are amazing birds ~~to see~~.

___/9 pts **E. Circle all conjunctions and underline interjections in the following sentences. (Review Lessons XVII and XVIII if you have questions.)**

(conjunctions are boxed)

a. Oh no! Mrs. Smith [and] Mrs. Leguard are here already. The cake [and] the pie
    are not ready [but] the coffee is.
b. Alas! The dog [and] cat do not get along [nor] does the horse play with the dog [or] cat.
c. Yikes! This class is almost over.

117

___/ 16 pts (if student marks articles as adjectives, remind him that those are adjectives we have not covered in this course, so go pick other adjectives. "Ice" on cream could be considered an adjective or just part of the noun.) **F. Find 11 adjectives and 5 pronouns in the following paragraph. (Review Lessons XXII and XXIV if you have questions.)**

Adjectives:

young	rough	delicious
dusty	tinkling	chocolate
old	black	happy
shiny	uninterested	

Pronouns:

He	you
it	I
whom	

The young boy skipped along the dusty, old road. He saw a shiny coin on the rough road near a tinkling brook. The boy picked it up. "To whom does the coin belong?" The boy looked around and saw a black crow. "Does the coin belong to you?"

"Caw!" said the uninterested crow and flew off.

"I can keep the coin and buy delicious chocolate ice cream!" said the happy boy.

___/9 pts **G. Put an "s" above all singular nouns and a "p" above all plural nouns. The nouns are underlined for you. (Review Lesson I if you have questions.)**

   P   S   S

Children, please play quietly. The baby is sleeping. Babies need to sleep to grow

               P   P   P   S

big. Baby birds, baby sheep, and baby kittens all sleep. "A baby sheep is called a

  S   S

lamb," Sally giggled.

/5 pts **H. Say whether the underlined words are the verb "to be" or a helping verb. (Review Lessons X and XVII if you have questions.)**

a. I <u>am</u> calling the dog.	helping verb	verb to be
b. I <u>am</u> happy.	helping verb	verb to be
c. The dog <u>is</u> big.	helping verb	verb to be
d. The children <u>are</u> playing.	helping verb	verb to be
e. I <u>will be</u> there soon.	helping verb	verb to be

____/12 pts **I. Does each verb express a complete (C) or incomplete (I) action? Is that action present, past or future? (Review Lesson IV if you have questions.)**

I was calling.	C	I		Past	Present	Future
I am calling.	C	I		Past	Present	Future
I will be calling.	C	I		Past	Present	Future
I have called.	C	I		Past	Present	Future
I had called.	C	I		Past	Present	Future
I will have called.	C	I		Past	Present	Future

____/4 pts **J. Is the verb active or passive? (Review Lesson II if you have questions.) (Remember: the subject does the action if the verb is active. The subject receives the action if the verb is passive.)**

a. Mary baked a cake.	Active	Passive
b. The cake was baked by Mary.	Active	Passive
c. Sam calls his friend.	Active	Passive
d. The dog was hit by the ball.	Active	Passive

____/ 3pts **K. Do each of the following sentences express a wish, a command, or a statement? (Review Lesson XXI if you have questions.)**

a. May God bless you.	<u>wish</u>
b. I ran in the race yesterday.	<u>statement</u>
c. Go to the store.	<u>command</u>

Final Review of Latin Grammar
෨෮෬

223 possible points   Student Score: _____

____/18 pts **A. What is the stem of these verbs? Circle it. (If you have any questions, please review Lesson III, IV, and V).**

orare	ponere	petere
munire	bibere	ducere
currere	credere	discere
venire	occupare	mittere
audire	gerere	mittere
scibere	venire	trahere

____/20 pts **B. What is the stem of these nouns? Circle the stem. What declension do they belong to? (If you have any questions, please review Lesson VI.)**

mons, montis (m) Declension: 3	collis, collis	Declension: 3
victoria, victoriae Declension: 1	servus, servi	Declension: 2
caedes, caedis Declension: 3	hostis, hostis	Declension: 3
salus, salutis Declension: 3	dominus, domini	Declension: 2
pecunia, pecuniae Declension: 1	periculum, periculi Declension: 2

____/4 pts **C. Decline the reflexive pronoun "--------, sui." (Review Lesson XXI if you have questions.)**

Nominative	Genitive	Dative	Accusative	Ablative
	sui	sibi	se	se

_____/84 pts **D. Conjugation the verbs fully. (You may wish to review a recent lesson or Lesson XIX if you have questions.)**

Fill in this chart. Use *currere*:

STEM: curre	Present	Past	Future Regulars	Subjunctive Present (aka Future Possible)
1st Singular	curro	currebam	curram	curram
2nd Singular	curris	currebas	curres	curras
3rd Singular	currit	currebat	curret	currat
1st Plural	currimus	currebamus	curremus	curramus
2nd Plural	curritis	currebatis	curretis	curratis
3rd Plural	currunt	currebant	current	currant

Fill in this chart. Use *audire*:

STEM: audi	Present	Past	Future Regulars	Subjunctive Present (aka Future Possible)
1st Singular	audio	audiebam	audiam	audiam
2nd Singular	audis	audiebas	audies	audias
3rd Singular	audit	audiebat	audiet	audiat
1st Plural	audimus	audiebamus	audiemus	audiamus
2nd Plural	auditis	audiebatis	audietis	audiatis
3rd Plural	audiunt	audiebant	audient	audiant

Fill in this chart. Use *sum*:

	Present	Past	Future Regulars
1st Singular	sum	eram	ero
2nd Singular	es	eras	eris
3rd Singular	est	erat	erit
1st Plural	sumus	eramus	erimus
2nd Plural	estis	eratis	eritis
3rd Plural	sunt	erant	erunt

Fill in this chart. Use *possum:*

	Present	Past	Future Regulars
1st Singular	possum	poteram	potero
2nd Singular	potes	poteras	poteris
3rd Singular	potest	poterat	poterit
1st Plural	possumus	poteramus	poterimus
2nd Plural	potestis	poteratis	poteritis
3rd Plural	possunt	poterant	poterunt

___92 pts **E. Decline the following nouns and adjectives (Review Lesson XVI, XIX, XXI, and XXIII if you have any questions.)**

Number	CASE	3rd Regular Masculine/Feminine	3rd I – stem Masculine/Feminine	3rd Regular Neuter	3rd I - stem Neuter
Singular	Nominative	crux	fons	nomen	mare
	Genitive	cruces	fontis	nominis	maris
	Dative	cruci	fonti	nomini	mari
	Accusative	crucem	fontem	nomen	mare
	Ablative	cruce	fonte	nomine	mari
Plural	Nominative	cruces	fontes	nomina	maria
	Genitive	crucum	fontium	nominum	marium
	Dative	crucibus	fontibus	nominibus	maribus
	Accusative	cruces	fontes	nomina	maria
	Ablative	crucibus	fontibus	nominibus	maribus

Fill in the chart with the phrase *fortis puella*:

Case	Singular	Plural
Nominative	fortis puella	fortes puellae
Genitive	fortis puellae	fortium puellarum
Dative	forti puellae	fortibus puellis
Accusative	fortem puellam	fortes puellas
Ablative	forti puella	fortibus puellis

Fill in the chart with the phrase *bonus dominus*:

Case	Singular	Plural
Nominative	bonus dominus	boni domini
Genitive	boni domini	bonorum dominorum
Dative	bono domino	bonis dominis
Accusative	bonum dominum	bonos dominos
Ablative	bono domino	bonis dominis

Fill in the chart with the phrase *ingens donum*:

Case	Singular	Plural
Nominative	ingens donum	intentia dona
Genitive	ingentis doni	ingentium donorum
Dative	ingenti dono	ingentibus donis
Accusative	ingens donum	ingentia dona
Ablative	ingenti dono	ingentibus donis

___/5 pts **F. Identify the following as adverbs, interjections, conjunctions, prepositions that take accusative, or prepositions that take the ablative. Do this by filling in the correct headers on each column. (If you have questions, the following lessons may help: Lesson XIII — prepositions, Lesson XVII — conjunctions, Lesson XVIII — interjections, Lesson XIX — adverbs)**

prepositions that take abl	prepositions that take acc	adverbs	interjections	conjunctions
in	trans	nunc	o	et
a, ab	contra	saepe	eheu	sed
cum	in	ubi		vel
e, ex	per	diu		
de	ad	non		

___/10 pts **G. Which of the following are i---stem? Which of the i ---stem rules apply to those words? (Review Lesson XVI if you have questions.)**

A noun is i – stem if it.....
Rule A: Ends in –is or –es in the nominative first form and has the same number of syllables in the first and second form.
Rule B: Ends in –s or –x in the nominative first form and has a stem that ends in two consonants
Rule C: Ends in –al, ---ar, or –e in the nominative first form (neuter nouns).

a. homo, hominis (m)   ___ i -- stem Rule: ____   X Regular

b. urbs, urbis   X i -- stem Rule: B   ___Regular

c. flumen, fluminis   ___i -- stem Rule: ____   X Regular

d. civitas, civitatis   ___i -- stem Rule: ____   X Regular

e. caedes, caedis   X i -- stem Rule: A   ___Regular

f. collis, collis (m)   X i -- stem Rule: A   ___Regular

g. pars, partis   X i -- stem Rule: B   ___Regular

h. agmen, agminis   ___i -- stem Rule: ____   X Regular

i. nomen, nominis   ___i -- stem Rule: ____   X Regular

j. mare, maris   X i -- stem Rule: C   ___Regular

125

Final Test of English Grammar

____student score (add bonus points to student score) /39

Our Father who are (in heaven,) holy is your name. May your kingdom come. May your will be done (on earth) as it is done (in heaven.) Give us this day our daily bread and forgive us our trespasses as we forgive those who trespass (against us.) Lead us not (into temptation) but deliver us (from the evil one.)

____/11 pts **I. Circle all verbs in the above paragraph.** (they are boxed) Add two bonus points if "may" is circled both times.

____/1 pts **II. How many sentences are there?** <u>5</u>

____/3 pts **III. Find a command, a wish, and a statement in the above paragraph:** Command: <u>Give us this day our daily bread and forgive us our trespasses…, lead us not into temptation, but deliver us from evil.</u>
Wish: <u>May your kingdom come, may your will be done on earth as it is in heaven.</u>
Statement: <u>Our Father who are in heaven, holy is your name.</u>

____/7 pts **IV. Put parentheses around every prepositional phrase.** Add one bonus point for not choosing "as."

____/2 pt **V. Find a conjunction in the last sentence:** <u>but</u>

____/11 **VI. List all nouns in the prayer:** Father, heaven, name, kingdom, will, earth, heaven, day, bread, trespasses, temptation, (if "one" is included, do not count it wrong.)

____/3 **VII. Find three adjectives — not including pronouns — in the above paragraph. (Hint: there is one in the first sentence.)** <u>holy, daily, evil</u>

____/1 **VIII. Does any sentence not have pronouns in it?**   Yes   No

Final Test of Latin Grammar

____Student Score/67 pts

____/15 pts **I. Identify the person (1st, 2nd, 3rd), tense (present, past, future, future possible), and number (singular, plural) of the following verbs:**

muniemus	Person: 1st	Number: pl	Tense: future
audiat	Person: 3rd	Number: s	Tense: future possible
regebas	Person: 2nd	Number: s	Tense: past
venietis	Person: 2nd	Number: pl	Tense: future
sunt	Person: 3rd	Number: pl	Tense: present

____/6 pts **II. Identify the case of each of the following nouns:**

collem	accusative	ablative	dative
flumina	ablative	dative	nominative
parti	genitive	nominative	dative
poetas	ablative	accusative	nominative
donum	nominative	dative	ablative
gentium	genitive	nominative	dative

____/4 pts **III. Put a smiley face next to the adjectives and their nouns that agree:**

☺ fortium pastorum   ☺ magna gratia
☺ ingentem gratiam   ____ forte victoria

___/42 pts **IV. Translate:**

If the student looked up vocabulary, the first five words looked up should not be counted as wrong, assuming the student uses the correct word.

a. Holy Mary seeks peace for Christians. ___/10 pts (one for correct vocab, one for correct ending)

Maria sancta pacem Christianibus petit.

b. Roma est urbs magna. ___/8 pts

Rome is a great city.

c. Caesar fortis pontem | trans | mare muniet. ___/11 pts (boxed word only worth one point)

Brave Caesar will build a bridge | across | the sea.

d. A great shout was coming | out of | the city of the evil tribe. ___/13 pts

Clamor magnus | ex | urbe gentis malae veniebat.

Vocabulary workspace — put down any words here that you need to look up. If you are looking up the Latin meanings of English nouns, remember to put down their first and second forms. You can look up five words without it affecting your grade. Look up other words if you need too. List them here too.

Latin-English Glossary

A

a, ab (abl)	by
acer/acris/acre, acris	bitter
ad (acc)	to, toward
ager, agri	field
agere	to do, act
agmen, agminis	column, army
amicus, amici	friend
ante (acc)	before
arbor, arboris (f)	tree
audire	to hear

B

bellum, belli	war
bibere	to drink
bonus, i/bona, ae/bonum, i	good
brevis, brevis/breve, brevis	short, brief

C

caedes, caedis	slaughter
caelum, caeli	heaven
Caesar, Caesaris	Caesar
Christus, Christi	Christ
Christianus, Christian	Christian
canis, canis (m/f)[1]	dog
caput, capitis	head
caritas, caritatis	love
cedere	to yield
Cicero, Ciceronis	Cicero
civis, civis (m/f)	citizen
civitas, civitatis	state

C (cont)

clamor, clamoris	shouting, shout
collis, collis (m)	hill
contra (acc)	against
copia, copiae	supply
corpus, corporis (n)	body
credere	to believe
crux, crucis	cross
cum (abl)	with
cur	why
currere	to run

D

de (abl)	from, down from, concerning
defendere	to defend
denique	finally
Deus, Dei	God
dicere	to speak, say
discere	to learn
diu	for a long time
dolor, doloris	sorrow
dominus, domini	lord
ducere	to lead
dux, ducis	leader

E

e, ex (abl)	out of
edere	to eat
eheu	alas
eques, equitis	horseman
et	and

F

filia, filiae	daughter
filius, filii	son
flumen, fluminis	river

---

[1] Canis, canis is an i stem word that over time lost its "I" in the genitive plural. In this course, we accept either "canum" or canium" as the genitive plural.

F (cont)

fons, fontis (m)	fountain
fortis/forte, fortis	brave
frumentum, frumenti	grain

G

Gallia, Galliae	France
Gallus, Galli	a Frenchman
gens, gentis	tribe
gerere	to wage
gladius, gladii	sword
gloria, gloriae	glory
gratia, gratiae	grace

H

hostis, hostis	enemy
homo, hominis	man

I

imperator, imperatoris	general, emperor
imperium, imperii	command, power, empire
in (acc)	into, onto
in (abl)	in, on
ingens, ingentis	huge
inopia, inopiae	scarcity, lack
iter, itineris (n)	journey

L

laudare	to praise
legio, legionis	legion
lex, legis	law
longus, i/longa, ae/longum, i long	
lux, lucis	light

M

magnus, i/magna, ae/magnum, i	great, large
malus, i/mala, ae/malum, i	evil
mare, maris	sea
Maria, Mariae	Mary
mater, matris	mother
miles, militis	soldier
mittere	to send
mons, montis (m)	mountain
mundus, mundi	world
munire	to fortify
murus, muri	wall

N

nauta, nautae	sailor
nomen, nominis	name
non	not
numerus, numeri	number
nunc	now

O

oratio, orationis	prayer
o!	oh!

P

panis, panis (m)[2]	bread
pars, partis	part
pastor, pastoris	shepherd
pater, patris	father
pax, pacis	peace
pecunia, pecuniae	money
per (acc)	through
periculum, periculi	danger
petere	to seek

---

[2] "Panis, panis" is like "Canis, canis" in terms of its genitive plural. Accept either "panium" or "panum" for plural genitive.

P (cont)

poeta, poetae	poet
ponere	to put, place
pons, pontis (m)	bridge
populus, populi	people
post (acc)	after
praemium, praemii	reward
princeps, principis	chief, leading man
provincia, provinciae	province

R

regere	to rule
regnum, regni	kingdom
rex, regis	king
Roma, Romae	Rome
Romanus, Romani	a Roman

S

saepe	often
salus, salutis	safety
sanctus, i/sancta, ae/sanctum, i	holy
scribere	to write
sed	but
semper	always
sentire	to feel
signum, signi	sign, standard
silva, silvae	forest
sol, solis (m)	sun

T

trahere	to draw
trans (acc)	across
tempus, temporis (n)	time
tentatio, tentationis	temptation
terra, terrae	land

U

ubi	where
urbs, urbis	city

V

vel	or
venire	to come
veritas, veritatis	truth
via, viae	road, way
victoria, victoriae	victory
vincere	to conquer
virgo, virginis	virgin
virtus, virtutis	virtue
vivere	to live
vox, vocis	voice
vulnus, vulneris (n)	wound

Pronunciation Guide

Vowel	LONG		SHORT	
Aa	ā	(father)	ă	(idea)
Ee	ē	(say)	ĕ	(net)
Ii	ī	(machine)	ĭ	(lit)
Oo	ō	(holy)	ŏ	(obey)
Uu	ū	(boot)	ŭ	(put)

Dipthongs

ae (ay)	ei (eight)	oe (boy) (Ecclesiastical: oh'ay)
eu (eh'oo)	au (ouch)	ui (oo'ee)

Consonants

- No second sound for "c" (cat) and "g" (get) in Classical Latin. In Ecclesiastical Latin, you can use the soft "g" (gentle) and a new sound for "c" (chain) before "ae", "e", "oe" or "i".
- "S" is always like "sea", never "ease".
- Consonant "I" is like "y" in young.
- Consonant "v" is like "w" in "wing" in Classical Latin only.

Every Latin word has as many syllables as it does vowels or diphthongs. English has silent letters, however in the Latin language each consonant, vowel and diphthong is pronounced separately.

Also note that a "ph" in Latin, should be pronounced as an "f".

English-Latin Glossary

A

across	trans (acc)
to act, to do	agere
after	post (acc)
against	contra (acc)
alas	eheu
always	semper
and	et
army, column	agmen, agminis

B

before	ante (acc)
to believe	credere
bitter	acer/acris/acre, acris
body	corpus, corporis (n)
brave	fortis/forte, fortis
bread	panis, panis (m)
bridge	pons, pontis (m)
brief, short	brevis, brevis/breve, brevis
but	sed
by	a, ab (abl)

C

Caesar	Caesar, Caesaris
Christ	Christus, Christi
Christian	Christianus, Christiani
Cicero	Cicero, Ciceronis
chief, leading man	princeps, principis
citizen	civis, civis (m/f)
city	urbs, urbis
column, army	agmen, agminis
to come	venire
command, power, empire	imperium, i
concerning, from, down from	de (abl)
to conquer	vincere
crux, crucis	cross

D

danger	periculum, periculi
daughter	filia, filiae
to defend	defendere
to do, to act	agere
dog	canis, canis (m/f)
down from, from concerning	de (abl)
to draw	trahere
to drink	bibere

E

to eat	edere
emperor, general	imperator, imperatoris
empire, power, command	imperium, imperii
enemy	hostis, hostis
evil	malus, i/mala, ae/malum, i

F

father	pater, patris
to feel	sentire
finally	denique
for a long time	diu
to fortify	munire
forest	silva, silvae
fountain	fons, fontis (m)
France	Gallia, Galliae
a Frenchman	Gallus, Galli
friend	amicus, amici
from, down from, concerning	de (ab)

G

general, emperor	imperator, imperatoris
glory	gloria, gloriae
God	Deus, Dei
good	bonus, i/bona, ae/bonum, i
grace	gratia, gratiae
grain	frumentum, frumenti
great, large	magnus, i/magna, ae/magnum, i

H

head	caput, capitis
to hear	audire
heaven	caelum, caeli
hill	collis, collis (m)
holy	sanctus, i/sancta, ae/sanctum, i
horseman	eques, equitis
huge	ingens, ingentis

I

in, on	in (abl)
into, onto	in (acc)

J

journey	iter, itineris (n)

K

king	rex, regis
kingdom	regnum, regni

L

lack, scarcity	inopia, inopiae
land	terra, terrae
large, great	magnus, i/magna, ae/magnum, i
law	lex, legis

L (cont)

to lead	ducere
leader	dux, ducis
leading man, chief	princeps, principis
to learn	discere
legion	legio, legionis
light	lux, lucis
to live	vivere
long	longus, i/longa, ae/longum, i
lord	dominus, domini
love	caritas, caritatis

M

man	homo, hominis
Mary	Maria, Mariae
money	pecunia, pecuniae
mother	mater, matris
mountain	mons, montis (m)

N

name	nomen, nominis
not	non
now	nunc
number	numerus, numeri

O

often	saepe
on, in	in (abl)
onto, into	in (acc)
or	vel
out of	e, ex (abl)

P

part	pars, partis
peace	pax, pacis
people	populus, populi
to place, put	ponere
poet	poeta, poetae
power, command, empire	imperium, imperii
to praise	laudare
prayer	oratio, orationis
to put, place	ponere

R

reward	praemium, praemii
river	flumen, fluminis
road, way	via, viae
a Roman	Romanus, Romani
Rome	Roma, Romae
to rule	regere
to run	currere

S

safety	salus, salutis
sailor	nauta, nautae
to say, speak	dicere
scarcity, lack	inopia, inopiae
sea	mare, maris
to seek	petere
to send	mittere
shepherd	pastor, pastoris
short, brief	brevis, brevis/breve, brevis
shouting, shout	clamor, clamoris
sign, standard	signum, signi
slaughter	caedes, caedis
soldier	miles, militis
son	filius, filii
sorrow	dolor, doloris
to speak, say	dicere

S (cont)

standard, sign	signum, signi
state	civitas, civitatis
sun	sol, solis (m)
supply	copia, copiae
sword	gladius, gladii

T

temptation	tentatio, tentationis
through	per (acc)
time	tempus, temporis (n)
to, toward	ad (acc)
tree	arbor, arboris (f)
tribe	gens, gentis
truth	veritas, veritatis

V

victory	victoria, victoriae
virgin	virgo, virginis
virtue	virtus, virtutis
voice	vox, vocis

W

to wage	gerere
wall	murus, muri
war	bellum, belli
way, road	via, viae
where	ubi
why	cur
with	cum (abl)
world	mundus, mundi
wound	vulnus, vulneris (n)
to write	scribere

Y

to yield	cedere

Vocabulary by Lesson

Lesson IV

agere	to do, act	petere	to seek
audire	to hear	ponere	to put, place
laudare	to praise	tenere	to hold
munire	to fortify		

Lesson V

bibere	to drink	discere	to learn
cedere	to yield	ducere	to lead
credere	to believe	mittere	to send
currere	to run	venire	to come
dicere	to speak, say		

Lesson VIII

agmen, agminis	column, army	Cicero, Ciceronis	Cicero
arbor, arboris (f)	tree	dux, ducis	leader
Caesar, Caesaris	Caesar	gens, gentis	tribe
canis, canis (m/f)	dog	pars, partis	part
caput, capitis	head	rex, regis	king
caritas, caritatis	love	virtus, virtutis	virtue

Lesson X

eques, equitis	horseman	urbs, urbis	city
lex, legis	law	veritas, veritatis	truth
lux, lucis	light	vox, vocis	voic
nomen, nominis	name		

Lesson XI

civis, civis	state	virgo, virginis	virgin
civitas, civitatis	citizen, citizenship	pastor, pastoris	shepherd
clamor, clamoris	shouting, shout	vivere	to live
vincere	to conquer		

Lesson XII

corpus, corporis (n)	body	pax, pacis	peace
flumen, fluminis	river	pons, pontis (m)	bridge
iter, itineris (n)	journey	vulnus, vulneris (n)	wound
pater, patris	father		

Lesson XIII

caedes, caedis	slaughter	mons, montis (m)	mountain
collis, collis (m)	hill	salus, salutis	safety
hostis, hostis	enemy		

Lesson XIV

a, ab (ablative)	by	e, ex (ablative)	out of
ad (accusative)	to, towards	in (accusative)	into, onto
ante (accusative)	before	in (ablative)	in, on
contra (accusative)	against	per (accusative)	through
cum (ablative)	with	post (accusative)	after
de (ablative)	from, down from, concerning	trans (accusative)	acr

homo, hominis	man	mater, matris	mother
imperator, imperatoris	general, emperor	miles, militis	soldier
legio, legionis	legion	princeps, principis	chief, leading man

Lesson XVI

defendere	to defend	fons, fontis (m)	fountain
dolor, doloris	sorrow	gerere	to wage
edere	to eat	mare, maris	sea

Lesson XVII

et	and	sol, solis (m)	sun
oratio, orationis	prayer	trahere	to draw
panis, panis (m)	bread	tempus, temporis (n)	time
regere	to rule	tentatio, tentationis	temptation
scribere	to write	vel	or
sed	but	crux, crucis	cross
sentire	to feel		

Lesson XVIII

Eheu!	Alas!	O!	Oh!

Lesson XX

cur	why	nunc	now
denique	finally	saepe	often
diu	for a long time	ubi	where
non	not	semper	always

Lesson XXI

copia, copiae	supply	inopia, inopiae	scarcity, lack
filia, filiae	daughter	Maria, Mariae	Mary
Gallia, Galliae	France	nauta, nautae (m)	sailor
gloria, gloriae	glory	pecunia, pecuniae	money
gratia, gratiae	grace	poeta, poetae (m)	poet

Lesson XXIV

amicus, amici	friend	gladius, gladii	sword
bellum, belli	war	imperium, imperii	command,
caelum, caeli	heaven		power, empire
Christus, Christi	Christ	mundus, mundi	world
Christianus, Christiani	Christian	murus, muri	wall
Deus, Dei	God	numerus, numeri	number
dominus, domini	lord	periculum, periculi	danger
filius, filii	son	praemium, praemii	reward
frumentum, frumenti	grain	populus, populi	people
Gallus, Galli	a Frenchman		

Lesson XXV

regnum, regni	kingdom	silva, silvae	forest
Roma, Romae	Rome	terra, terrae	land, earth
Romanus, Romani	a Roman	via, viae	road, way
signum, signi	sign, standard	victoria, victoriae	victory

Lesson XXVI

acer/acris/acre, acris	bitter
difficilis/difficile, difficilis	difficult
fortis/forte, fortis	brave
ingens, ingentis	huge
bonus, i/bona, ae/bonum, i	good
longus, i/longa, ae/longum, i	long
magnus, i/magna, ae/magnum, i	great, large
malus, i/mala, ae/malum, i	evil
sanctus, i/sancta, ae/sanctum, i	holy

Chart of Special Forms

sum, es, est, sumus, estis, sunt *(I am, you are, he is, we are, you are, they are)***eram, eras, erat, eramus, eratis, erant** *(I was, you were, he was, we were, you were, they were)***ero, eris, erit, erimus, eritis, erunt** *(I will be, you will be, he will be, we will be, you will be, they will be)*

possum, potes, potest, possumus, potestis, possunt *(I am able, you are able, he is able, we are able, you are able, they are able)*

poteram, poteras, poterat, poteramus, poteratis, poterant *(I was able, you were able, he was able, we were able, you were able, they were able)*

potero, poteris, poterit, poterimus, poteritis, poterunt *(I will be able, you will be able, he will be able, we will be able, you will be able, they will be able)*

Fundamentals 1 Translation Exercises
Answer Key

Lesson 10

If you are having trouble translating the more complex sentences that have been introduced in this lesson, then follow these steps to do **Additional Exercise C**.

Example Sentence: *The leader defends the king.*	
Step 1: Circle the subject and predicate nominative; underline the direct object. Cross out the words "the," "a," and "an."	A. dux, ducis defendere rex, regis ~~The~~ (leader) defends ~~the~~ <u>king</u>.
Step 2: Write the Latin word you would use on line A. Write the word as it is given to you in your vocabulary list.	B. <u>defende</u> <u>reg</u> C. <u>Dux</u> <u>defendit</u> <u>regem.</u>
Step 3: Write the stem of the Latin words on line B (for those words that you will need the stem).	
Step 4: Add the correct endings on line C to complete the translation.	

Why do you think that you are asked to write the Latin word as it is given to you in your vocabulary? Remember, the first form for nouns gives you the nominative, but the second form is what you use to find the stem. The infinitive for verbs is also what you use to find the verb stem.

On line B you are not given a spot to give a stem for "dux, ducis." Why not? Because subjects take the nominative case (the first form). So you don't need a stem to get the right translation.

Use these steps to translate the sentences on the next page.

1. The leader was conquering Caesar.	
Step 1: Circle the subject and predicate nominative; underline the direct object. Cross out the words "the," "a," and "an."	A. dux, ducis vincere Caesar, Caesaris ~~The~~ (leader) was conquering <u>Caesar</u>.
Step 2: Write the Latin word you would use on line A. Write the word as it is given to you in your vocabulary list.	B. vince Caesar C. Dux vincebat Caesarem.
Step 3: Write the stem of the Latin words on line B (for those words that you will need the stem).	Remember "was conquering" is the verb! It is one word in Latin. Put it in the past tense.
Step 4: Add the correct endings on line C to complete the translation.	

2. The shepherd sends the dog.	
Step 1: Circle the subject and predicate nominative; underline the direct object. Cross out the words "the," "a," and "an."	A. pastor, pastoris mittere canis, canis ~~The~~ (shepherd) sends <u>the</u> <u>dog</u>.
Step 2: Write the Latin word you would use on line A. Write the word as it is given to you in your vocabulary list.	B. mitte can C. Pastor mittit canem.
Step 3: Write the stem of the Latin words on line B (for those words that you will need the stem).	
Step 4: Add the correct endings on line C to complete the translation.	

3. The leader is a tree.	
Step 1: Circle the subject and predicate nominative; underline the direct object. Cross out the words "the," "a," and "an."	A. _dux, ducis_ (use irregular "to be" verb) _arbor, arboris_ The~~~~ (leader) is ~~a~~ (tree.)
Step 2: Write the Latin word you would use on line A. Write the word as it is given to you in your vocabulary list.	B. *No stems for this sentence*
Step 3: Write the stem of the Latin words on line B (for those words that you will need the stem).	C. _Dux_ _est_ _arbor._
Step 4: Add the correct endings on line C to complete the translation.	

Lesson 12

In this lesson you are asked to do some complex Latin-to-English sentences. Going from Latin to English is much easier than going from English to Latin, because the endings are already on the words. You just have to remember what those endings mean.

Use these steps to translate the sentences in **Additional Exercise B.**

Example Sentence: Caesar defendit Ciceronem.	
Step 1: Line A is for nouns. Write which case each of the nouns is in. Line B is for verbs. Write which tense, person, and number the verb is.	Caesar defendit Ciceronem. A. <u>nominative</u> <u>accusative</u>
Step 2: Look up any vocabulary words you are not sure about and write them on line C.	B. <u>present, third person, singular</u> C. <u>defendere – to defend</u>
Step 3: Use the information you have from steps 1 and 2 to translate the sentence on line D.	D. <u>Caesar defends Cicero.</u>

---

1. Caesaris pater montem cedebat.	
Step 1: Line A is for nouns. Write which case each of the nouns is in. Line B is for verbs. Write which tense, person, and number the verb is.	Caesaris pater montem cedebat. *A. genitive nominative accusative*
Step 2: Look up any vocabulary words you are not sure about and write them on line C.	*B. past tense, third person, singular* C. _____
Step 3: Use the information you have from steps 1 and 2 to translate the sentence on line D.	*D. Caesar's father was yielding the mountain.*

2. Sum rex.	
Step 1: Line A is for nouns. Write which case each of the nouns is in. Line B is for verbs. Write which tense, person, and number the verb is.	Sum rex. *A. nominative* *B. present tense, first person, singular*
Step 2: Look up any vocabulary words you are not sure about and write them on line C.	C. _____
Step 3: Use the information you have from steps 1 and 2 to translate the sentence on line D.	*D. I am a king.*

3. Dux munit urbem virgini.	
Step 1: Line A is for nouns. Write which case each of the nouns is in. Line B is for verbs. Write which tense, person, and number the verb is.	Dux munit urbem virgini. *A. nominative accusative dative* *B. present tense, third person, singular*
Step 2: Look up any vocabulary words you are not sure about and write them on line C.	C. _____
Step 3: Use the information you have from steps 1 and 2 to translate the sentence on line D.	*D. The leader builds a city for the virgin.*

4. Pastor canem mittit.	
Step 1: Line A is for nouns. Write which case each of the nouns is in. Line B is for verbs. Write which tense, person, and number the verb is.	Pastor canem mittit. *A. nominative accusative* *B. present tense, third person, singular*
Step 2: Look up any vocabulary words you are not sure about and write them on line C.	C. _____
Step 3: Use the information you have from steps 1 and 2 to translate the sentence on line D.	*D. The shepherd sends a dog.*

Lesson 14

Use the same steps to translate **Additional Exercises C and D**. For Exercise D, there will be more parts to Step A, since you have learned many more uses of nouns, . Make sure you figure out what use of the noun each noun is before you begin to translate.

C. Latin-to-English

1. Ducam Caesaris agminem.	
Step 1: Line A is for nouns. Write which case each of the nouns is in. Line B is for verbs. Write which tense, person, and number the verb is.	Ducam Caesaris agminem. *A.* *genitive* *accusative*
Step 2: Look up any vocabulary words you are not sure about and write them on line C.	*B. future tense, first person, singular* C. _____
Step 3: Use the information you have from steps 1 and 2 to translate the sentence on line D.	*D. I will lead Caesar's army.*

2. Virgo bibit.	
Step 1: Line A is for nouns. Write which case each of the nouns is in. Line B is for verbs. Write which tense, person, and number the verb is.	Virgo bibit. *A. nominative*
Step 2: Look up any vocabulary words you are not sure about and write them on line C.	*B. present tense, third person, singular* C. _____
Step 3: Use the information you have from steps 1 and 2 to translate the sentence on line D.	*D. The virgin drinks.*

3. Caesar dicebat gentibus.	
Step 1: Line A is for nouns. Write which case each of the nouns is in. Line B is for verbs. Write which tense, person, and number the verb is.	Caesar dicebat gentibus. *A. nominative dative* *B. past tense, third person, singular*
Step 2: Look up any vocabulary words you are not sure about and write them on line C.	C. _____
Step 3: Use the information you have from steps 1 and 2 to translate the sentence on line D.	*D. Caesar was speaking to the tribes.*

4. Audies flumen.	
Step 1: Line A is for nouns. Write which case each of the nouns is in. Line B is for verbs. Write which tense, person, and number the verb is.	Audies flumen. *A. accusative* *B. future tense, second person, singular*
Step 2: Look up any vocabulary words you are not sure about and write them on line C.	C. _____
Step 3: Use the information you have from steps 1 and 2 to translate the sentence on line D.	*D. You will hear the river.*

Now that you have had some practice translating Latin-to-English using these steps, you will be asked to simply use your workbook to translate Latin-to-English. You are only given one line in your workbook, but you can use any extra space around your sentences to jot down notes that will help you. If it helps, mark above each noun its case, and above each verb its tense, number, and person. Then carefully translate each word.

D. English to Latin

1. The dog was hearing Cicero.	
Step 1: Circle subjects and predicate nominatives; underline direct objects; dash underline indirect objects; put a box around possessives. Put parentheses around prepositional phrases and write "abl" above the phrase if the preposition takes the ablative case and "acc" if it takes the accusative case. Cross out the words "the," "a," and "an."	A. *canis, canis* *audire* *Cicero, Ciceronis* ~~The~~ (dog) was hearing <u>Cicero.</u> B. *audi* *Ciceron* C. *Canis* *audiebat* *Ciceronem.*
Step 2: Write the Latin word you would use on line A. Write the word as it is given to you in your vocabulary list.	
Step 3: Write the stem of the Latin words on line B (for those words that you will need the stem).	
Step 4: Add the correct endings on line C to complete the translation.	

2. The tribes will come to Caesar.

Step 1: Circle subjects and predicate nominatives; underline direct objects; dash underline indirect objects; put a box around possessives. Put parentheses around prepositional phrases and write "abl" above the phrase if the preposition takes the ablative case and "acc" if it takes the accusative case. Cross out the words "the," "a," and "an."	A. *gens, gentis* *venire* *ad* *Caesar, Caesaris* The (tribes) will come (to Caesar.) ᵃᶜᶜ B. *veni* *Caesar* C. *Gens* *venient* *ad* *Caesarem.* Hint: is the "to" in this sentence an "ad" preposition + accusative or an indirect object?
Step 2: Write the Latin word you would use on line A. Write the word as it is given to you in your vocabulary list.	
Step 3: Write the stem of the Latin words on line B (for those words that you will need the stem).	
Step 4: Add the correct endings on line C to complete the translation.	

3. The tribes will come for Cicero.

Step 1: Circle subjects and predicate nominatives; underline direct objects; dash underline indirect objects; put a box around possessives. Put parentheses around prepositional phrases and write "abl" above the phrase if the preposition takes the ablative case and "acc" if it takes the accusative case. Cross out the words "the," "a," and "an."	A. *gens, gentis* *venire* *Cicero, Ciceronis* ~~The~~ (tribes) will come <u>for</u> Cicero. B. *veni* *Ciceron* C. *Gentes* *venient* *Ciceroni.*
Step 2: Write the Latin word you would use on line A. Write the word as it is given to you in your vocabulary list.	
Step 3: Write the stem of the Latin words on line B (for those words that you will need the stem).	
Step 4: Add the correct endings on line C to complete the translation.	

Lesson 15

Use the steps you have learned to translate **sentence D of Additional Exercise D.**

Step 1: Circle subjects and predicate nominatives; underline direct objects; dash underline indirect objects; put a box around possessives. Put parentheses around prepositional phrases and write "abl" above the phrase if the preposition takes the ablative case and "acc" if it takes the accusative case. **Draw an arrow under the appositive to the word it modifies.** Cross out the words "the," "a," and "an."
Step 2: Write the Latin word you would use on line A. Write the word as it is given to you in your vocabulary list.
Step 3: Write the stem of the Latin words on line B (for those words that you will need the stem).
Step 4: Add the correct endings on line C to complete the translation.

---

1. The man will seek the safety of the state against the enemy, Caesar.

A. *homo, hominis; petere; salus, salutis; civitas, civitatis; contra; hostis, hostis; Caesar, Caesaris*

acc

~~The~~ (man) will seek ~~the~~ safety [of ~~the~~ state] (against ~~the~~ enemy), Caesar.

B.   *pete   salut   civitat   host   Caesar*

C. *Homo petet salutem civitatis contra hostem, Caesarem.*

Lesson 16

Use these steps to do **Additional Exercise D Sentences A and B.** This time you are not given separate spaces for each word, but just one long line. Think carefully about what vocabulary words you need (for example, is this "to" an indirect object or an "ad"?) and which words you need stems for. The verbs are done for you in this exercise.

Step 1: Circle subjects and predicate nominatives; underline direct objects; dash underline indirect objects; put a box around possessives. Put parentheses around prepositional phrases and write "abl" above the phrase if the preposition takes the ablative case and "acc" if it takes the accusative case. **Draw an arrow under the appositive to the word it modifies.** Cross out the words "the," "a," and "an."

Step 2: Write the Latin word you would use on line A. Write the word as it is given to you in your vocabulary list.

Step 3: Write the stem of the Latin words on line B (for those words that you will need the stem).

Step 4: Add the correct endings on line C to complete the translation.

---

1. Caesar seeks peace for the tribes.

A. Caesar, Caesaris; petere; pax, pacis; gens, gentis

(Caesar)   seeks   peace   for   the   tribes.

B. pete, gent

C. Caesar petit pacem gentibus.

2. The leader of the army was running to the river. (use "agmen" for "army")

A. dux, ducis; agmen, agminis; currere; ad; flumen, fluminis

~~The~~ (leader) of ~~the~~ army was running (to ~~the~~ river.)

B. agmin, curre, flumin

C. Dux agminis currebat ad flumen.

Lesson 18

This time, you are only given two lines to do the translation on. The first line is for any notes you need about vocabulary words or stems. The second line is for the translation.

Step 1: Circle subjects and predicate nominatives; underline direct objects; dash underline indirect objects; put a box around possessives. Put parentheses around prepositional phrases and write "abl" above the phrase if the preposition takes the ablative case and "acc" if it takes the accusative case. Draw an arrow under the appositive to the word it modifies. Cross out the words "the," "a," and "an."
Step 2: Write any notes about vocabulary words or stems on line A.
Step 3: Write your translation on line B.

1. The (rivers) run (to the sea.)

A. _____

B. *Flumina currunt ad mare.*

2. (Cicero and Caesar) will eat bread (with the citizen.)

A. _____

B. *Cicero et Caesar edent panem cum cive.*

3. The (enemy) of the tribe was coming (to the city.)

A. _____

B. *Hostis gentis veniebat ad urbem.*

Lesson 19

Use these steps to do **Additional Exercise D sentences A and B.**

Step 1: Circle subjects and predicate nominatives; underline direct objects; dash underline indirect objects; put a box around possessives. Put parentheses around prepositional phrases and write "abl" above the phrase if the preposition takes the ablative case and "acc" if it takes the accusative case. Draw an arrow under the appositive to the word it modifies. Cross out the words "the," "a," and "an."
Step 2: Write any notes about vocabulary words or stems on line A.
Step 3: Write your translation on line B.

1. ~~The~~ (shepherd) was drinking (from ~~the~~ fountain.)
A. _____
B. *Pastor bibebat ex fonte.*

2. Now ~~the~~ (general) hastens ~~the~~ slaughter of ~~the~~ enemies' legion.
A. _____
B. *Nunc imperator contendit caedem legionis hostium.*

By now, you should be comfortable translating in your Fundamentals workbook. There you are given only one line and no special steps, but you now know how to carefully think through your sentences so that you get the right translation. If you need to make little notes to yourself next to the sentence, feel free to do so. If it helps you to circle subjects, underline direct objects, etc., do that too. You can always cut out "Step 1" from this worksheet of this book and tape it on your desk or put it on your bulletin board for future reference.